MICROSOFT OFFICE 365 NON-TECH SAVVY BIBLE 10 IN 1

From Beginner to Pro with This Fully Illustrated Guide– Word, Excel, PowerPoint, Access, Outlook, Skype, Teams, OneDrive, OneNote and Publisher

ALAN NORWOOD

Table of Contents

 22°C Sunny Search  W X P A O S T N P 09:00 AM 01/09/202

Section 4: Microsoft ACCESS 126

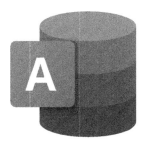

Section 5: Microsoft OUTLOOK 143

22°C
Sunny

🔍 Search

09:00 AM
01/09/202

Section 9:
Microsoft ONENOTE 201

Section 10:
Microsoft PUBLISHER....... 221

GET YOUR FREE BOOK BONUSES NOW!

(DOWNLOAD FOR FREE WITH THE BELOW INSTRUCTION!)

Do you want to unlock complete knowledge about Microsoft Office 365 Suite?

1. **Bonus 1: 300+ Excel Templates**
   Business - Personal - Project - Tracker - Chart - Invoice List - Calendar - Analysis Schedule - Budget

2. **Bonus 2: A Guide to Time Management**

3. **Bonus 3: A Guide to Productivity Management**

4. **Bonus 4: Advice on How to Prepare for a Job Interview**

5. **Bonus 5: How to Quickly Improve your Office 365 Skills**

<u>SCAN THE QR CODE</u> BELOW AND UNLOCK THE FULL POTENTIAL OF MICROSOFT OFFICE 365 SUITE!

22°C
Sunny

🔍 Search

09:00 AM
01/09/202

INSTRUCTION ON HOW TO UNLOCK
YOUR FREE BONUSES

ONLY 2 SIMPLE STEPS TO UNLOCK YOUR FREE BONUSES:

1. **Scan the QR code on the previous page** and unlock full knowledge of Office 365 Suite. Start now boost your knowledge!

2. **Let me know how you are excited about all the contents!** I look forward to your opinion on the book and the bonus content!

SCAN THE QR CODE BELOW AND LEAVE A QUICK REVIEW ON AMAZON TO SHARE YOUR THOUGHTS ON THIS BOOK.

The best way to do it? Simple! ***You can upload a brief video*** *with your thoughts. I will greatly appreciate an honest opinion about the book!*

Don't you want to create a video? Don't worry! ***You can do a short review with some photos*** *of dishes made thanks to this book or take photos of the most beautiful parts of the book.*

NOTE: You don't have to feel obligated, but it would be highly appreciated!

10 22°C Sunny Search W X P A O S T N P 09:00 AM 01/09/202

Introduction

Have you ever contemplated the hypothetical scenario of a computer lacking the presence of software applications such as Word, Excel, or PowerPoint? If an individual's birth year falls after 1990, it is unlikely that they would have encountered the suite, given it was introduced by Microsoft specifically for use with the Windows operating system during that time. Since its first launch, the software applications have been distributed through various mediums, including floppy disks, CD-ROMs, and more recently, via internet downloads accompanied by a unique serial number. The programs have undergone several updates and modifications over time, resulting in the current iteration that is in use today.

After introducing the aforementioned three primary programs, Microsoft proceeded to expand its software offerings to cater to many domains of operation. The program has transitioned from a hardware-based system to a cloud-based platform, facilitating online integration between each component. The interconnectivity across the many tools within the Microsoft Suite is a significant attribute, facilitating the seamless integration and utilization of their respective functionalities. One such use is utilizing an Excel spreadsheet to visually represent a computation within a Word document or a PowerPoint presentation that is being developed.

Due to the myriad capabilities and inherent advantages offered by these programs, they have served as the foundation for subsequent software applications now in use, exemplified as Google Documents. Upon careful examination of the accessible buttons inside each of these comparable apps, it becomes apparent that they have a striking resemblance to one another. The rationale behind this phenomenon may be attributed to the widespread adoption and dominance of the Office Suite, which served as the prevailing and exclusive software option for a considerable period. Consequently, it set the framework and defined the benchmarks for further developments in the field. The ribbon, which is currently recognized as the toolbar located at the top of the page, has established itself as the prevailing standard for navigating and utilizing these software applications.

Nevertheless, although the purpose of this discussion is not to go into the historical background of Microsoft Office, it is crucial to emphasize its significance due to the fact that nearly every contemporary occupation necessitates proficiency in using these software applications. Although some individuals are able to navigate these fundamental processes effortlessly, many of their intricacies often go unnoticed unless one commits to thoroughly investigating each of them. However, there is no need for concern since this book will provide comprehensive instruction on how to acquire expertise in utilizing these technologies.

It is worth noting that Excel possesses a vast array of over 1,000 calculating operations, with several other capabilities. Similarly, Word extends beyond its conventional perception as a document authoring application, offering users a multitude of additional options. In addition, it is worth noting the potential for generating dynamic presentations in PowerPoint and developing user-friendly applications in Access. The Microsoft Suite offers a wide range of options to users and continues to maintain its dominance in the market due to its enhanced capabilities. It remains the most widely utilized software package for both corporate and personal purposes.

22°C
Sunny

🔍 Search

09:00 AM
01/09/202

SHORTCUT FEATURES

The successful implementation of shortcut functions played a pivotal role in contributing to the benefits that Microsoft Office enjoyed. Prior to their implementation, users were required to input code in order to format their papers using a software application known as WordPerfect. Additionally, it should be noted that a significant number of computer users did not possess a mouse, since this peripheral device was very expensive and not widely accessible. The introduction of the shortcut function at the product launch was highly successful due to its ability to provide users an alternative to the mouse and streamline processes through automation, resulting in significant customer interest.

It is noteworthy that these apps offer a wide range of keyboard shortcuts, exceeding a total of 100. When utilizing Microsoft Windows on a personal computer, the operating system may be accessed by depressing the Ctrl key on the keyboard in conjunction with other supplementary keys, depending on the desired operation to be executed. In the case of owning a MacOS, the method of accessing shortcuts differs slightly, since it involves hitting the Cmd or Command button in conjunction with the corresponding key associated with the desired function. In all scenarios, the supplementary keys have the potential to encompass numerical digits, alphabetical characters, or even modifier keys like Shift.

If one lacks awareness or understanding of the subject matter at hand, there is no need for concern. Upon perusing each area, a compilation of the most prevalent shortcuts for the respective software will be encountered. In addition to that, one will get knowledge on the distinctive attributes that distinguish each program, encompassing both fundamental and advanced aspects, so providing a comprehensive learning experience. Are you prepared to begin your educational journey and acquire expertise in the field of program management?

Section 1:
Microsoft WORD

If you want to generate a paper, compile a report, or produce printable labels, Microsoft Word is the recommended software suite to employ. One often employed instrument among students is utilized for the purpose of conducting a thesis, among other applications, and for the creation and modification of text-based documents. Nevertheless, it should be noted that this capability is not limited just to this function. This application provides users with a wide array of options that include several purposes, including professional endeavors such as crafting resumes and promotional materials for restaurants, as well as personal endeavors like designing invites, scheduling books, and generating party posters.

If one was previously uninformed of the capabilities of Microsoft Word, there is no need for concern. The initial chapter provides instruction on optimizing one's circumstances. The course will start by covering fundamental concepts before progressing to more complex functionalities. Continue reading to acquire further knowledge about the subject matter.

STARTING WITH THE FUNDAMENTALS

Upon initiating the software, the user will be presented with a window prompt inquiring about their desired action. The available choices encompass the initiation of a fresh, unformatted document, as well as the provision of many suggested templates. Additionally, this feature will enable users to conveniently access recently accessed papers and make reference to any pinned documents. The initial crucial aspect that necessitates attention is as follows: If this document is often accessed, it is advisable to choose the pin icon located adjacent to the most recent change date of the document. This action will ensure that the document remains visible on the list at all times. The primary rationale for this is because, when the number of documents accessed increases, only the most recently accessed ones are displayed on the opening screen. Consequently, it would be advantageous to include a hyperlink to the often utilized documents.

There will be the following choices on the blue vertical bar on the left: You are currently on the page known as "**Home**," You can use the buttons **New** to start a brand-new blank document and **Open** to look for compatible files on your computer. You will find three further links at the bottom of this bar: **Account**, **Feedback**, and **Options**. You can see your account settings and determine whether any adjustments are required by clicking on the first link. Minor configuration options are also available, such as the ability to modify the theme and backdrop.

Subsequently, there is the feedback connection, characterized by its straightforward nature. The feature permits users to express their approval, disapproval, or offer suggestions for enhancing the program. Ultimately, the choices button will afford you the opportunity to personalize your settings pertaining to the utilization of Word. In this interface, users have the option to input their personal identification, specify their desired proofing methods for document review, select their language preferences, and designate the default file extension for saving purposes.

An additional benefit is the ability to customize the ribbon, referred to as the toolbar located at the uppermost section of the window. However, further elaboration on this topic will be provided shortly..

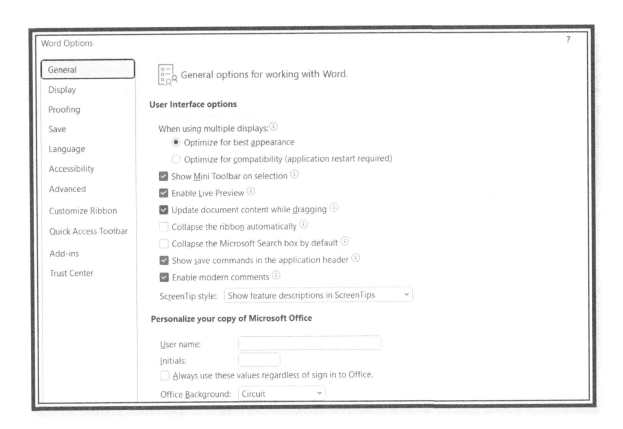

We will choose the '**new**' document option for this initial illustration. When you do, a toolbar will be visible at the top of a blank page. This is how making a new file will get started. Let's start by looking at the so-called ribbon and all the things that may be done with it.

The Ribbon

Now that you know what each section of the Word ribbon contains, you can quickly go there. As each of them will be fully discussed in the following sections of this chapter, this will only serve as an introduction. It is also crucial to note that the majority of the features you will see throughout the chapter have shortcuts, and you can find instructions on how to utilize them at the end of the chapter for quicker reference.

When you first open the new document, you'll see a bar at the top with many options. If this does not appear, move your cursor over the blue menu at the top of the page, and it should slide down. You may adjust this in Word so that it is always visible. Simply click on the pin in the ribbon's upper-right corner to accomplish this. If you prefer the opposite and want to hide it, click on the arrow in the same location.

Ribbon

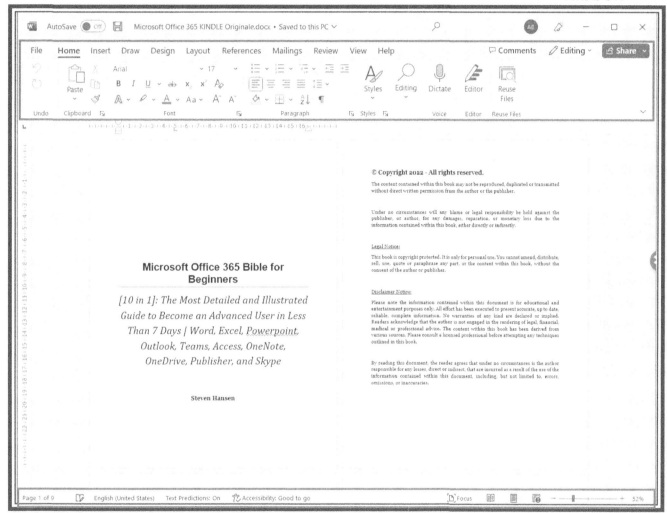

Status Bar

The first choice you'll have is related to the **file**. Although it has more options, the page that will open is similar to the main page. It will give users the option to begin, open, save, export, or print a document. We will move on to the next features as we already looked at these options in the previous section.

The next option on the ribbon is the **home section**. This will allow you to format the document according to your preferences. It is typically divided into five sections: **clipboard**, **font**, **paragraph**, and **styles**. You can **paste**, **cut**, **copy**, or use **format painter** in the clipboard area. The last one is a tool that allows the user to format any portion of text and make it consistent with the rest.

Home Tab

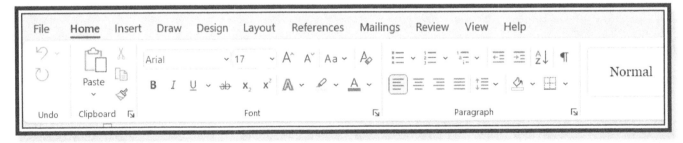

While writing, you can format your font in the **font section**. This section permits the selection of the desired font. You can also change the font's boldness, italics, underlining, and highlighting, as well as its color and size.

The paragraph feature enables you to create numbered or bulleted lists, adjust the text's indentation, arrange it in alphabetical order for lists, determine the line spacing, and even configure table design. The section that follows is the style section that will allow you to standardize the titles and subtitles of your text and will also be a valuable resource when creating tables of contents. In the final section, the editing area, the user will be able to search for words or phrases, replace content, and select specific words from the text.

Insert is the next item on the tab. As the name suggests, this allows you to add specific elements to documents. This includes **images and shapes**, as well as a header and footer. **It is separated into ten sections, including pages, tables, illustrations, add-ins, media, links**, comments, header and footer, text, and symbols. The user will be able to edit links and add videos to their documents. It also enables the creation and editing of equations without the need for hand calculations. This feature is useful for those looking to add value to their document by incorporating non-native software elements.

Insert Tab

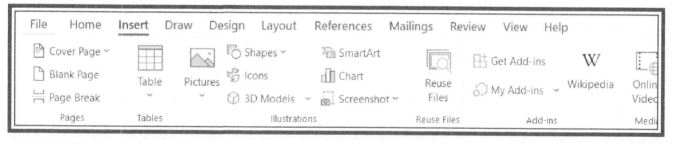

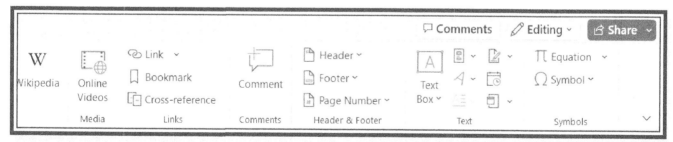

In the **design feature**, Word will allow you to create a file that has a specific design based on its set standards. Without having to format the document by hand, you can do so quickly here. The option to add color to the page background or borders is another bonus feature.

Finally, this tab offers the watermark feature, which is helpful for those who want to distribute controlled documents. Here, the user can choose what information should be included in the watermark and the format it should take, adding value for drafts, for instance.

Design Tab

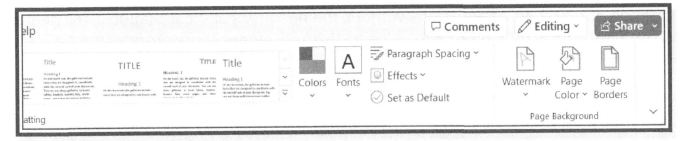

All the settings you want to make for the page of your document are referred to by the layout item on the menu. The user can choose the precise length they want for the indentation or how much space should be provided between the lines, and you can choose whether you want it to be in a landscape or portrait layout and whether you want to **divide your text into columns**.

This feature adds more detail to the paragraph section that we first saw in the home button. When adding an image to the text, you can choose here where it should be aligned and whether it should appear in front of the text or in the background.

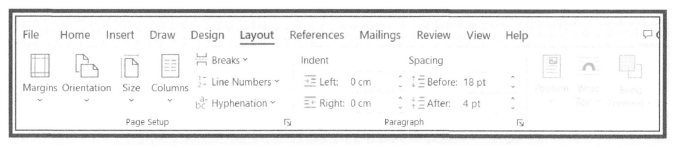

Layout Tab

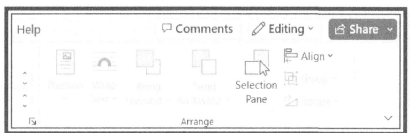

If you intend to write a book or a thesis, for instance, **the references section** will facilitate your work. **This section contains a table of contents, footnotes, research, citations, and bibliography, captions, an index, and a table of authorities**.

As you will see later in this chapter, it will be easier to create a table of contents if you use the title feature presented in the home area. It will also format your citations and bibliography in 12 distinct formats, including APA and Harvard. It also permits the addition of indexes, the creation of a table of authorities on the subject, and the insertion of captions within the document.

References Tab

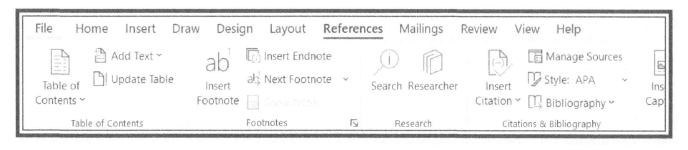

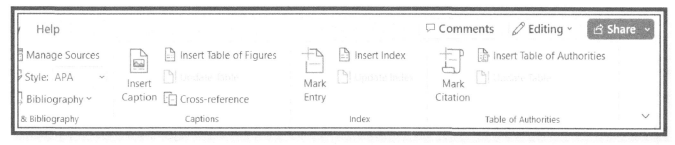

If you intend to use Word as a business tool, the next feature, **mailing**, can be particularly intriguing. This is because it will assist you in creating mailing lists and labels to facilitate your process. This section of the ribbon is separated into **create, begin mail merge, write and insert fields, preview results, and complete**. Imagine being able to print labels with the addresses of every friend to whom you wish to send a Christmas card. With Microsoft Word, this will be much simpler and faster; simply print and paste!

Mailings Tab

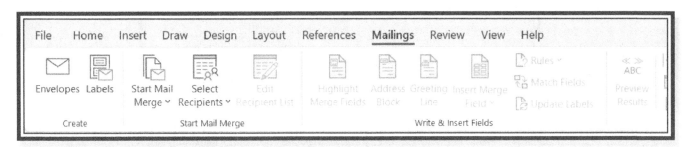

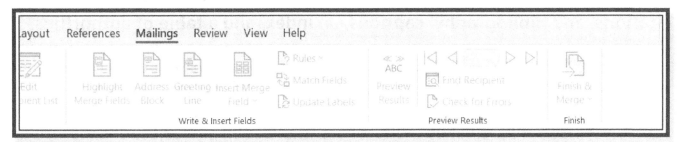

Assuming you have completed the document, the next item in the toolbar will assist you in editing and reviewing it. This section contains tools for **proofreading, accessibility, language, comments, tracking, changes, comparing, protecting, inking, and integrating content with OneNote.**

Review Tab

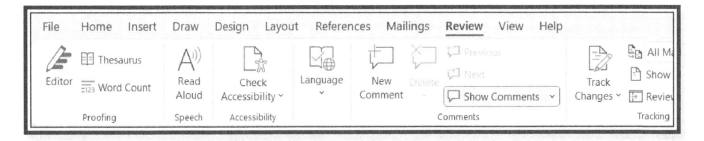

22°C
Sunny

Search

09:00 AM
01/09/202

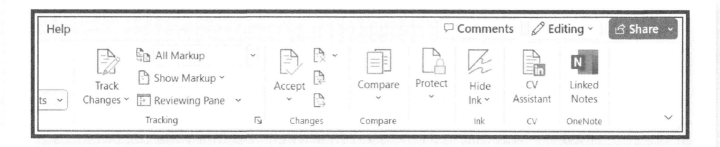

Using the tools in this tab, you can, for instance, proofread a document and make tracked changes so the author can see where you've made changes, add comments without altering the text, and even translate it into your preferred language. The ability to compare two documents is an additional feature that makes this site appealing. This means that if the person who read and edited the file you sent them did not track their changes, you will be able to identify them by comparing the original and the received document.

The **view** option is the final option on the tab before the help option. This will allow you to customize the document's appearance on your computer. It is divided into seven sections for this purpose: **views, page movement, show, zoom, window, macros, and SharePoint integration.** In this section, the user can also choose whether or not to display the ruler on the top and sides of the page, how much zoom to apply to the document, and whether or not to split the view into two windows to simultaneously view two parts of the same file.

View Tab

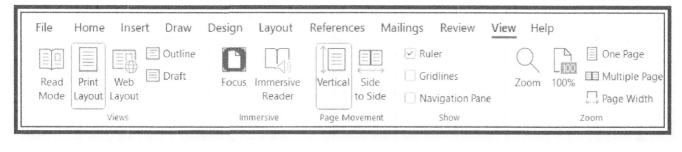

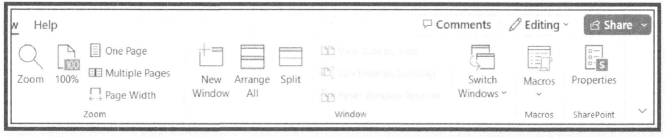

Despite the fact that these are the functional elements of the ribbon, there is one more element that is self-explanatory: the **help button**. It gives the user the option to contact support, provide feedback, and ask questions regarding program usage or how to perform specific tasks. In case you have any questions about how to use certain features, you can also access a small training feature. This is the final item on the toolbar at the top. However, you may have noticed that when you open the document, a thin gray line with some information appears at the bottom. Let's investigate its meaning.

Help Tab

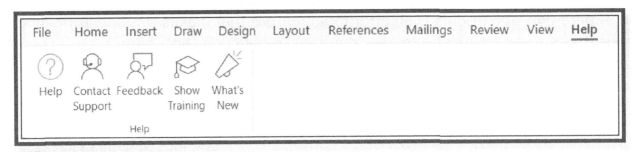

The Status Bar

This section is known as the status bar, and it provides access to some of the most important document information. The number of pages will be the first item displayed. You will be informed not only of the total number of pages in your document, but also of the **current page in the format page x of x**. This allows the user to quickly determine the document's size.

The following piece of information is also quite useful, especially for those who are writing within a word limit: the document's total word count. Initially, you may believe that this is a simple function that displays the number of words you have written. Nonetheless, knowing how many words are contained in a section relative to the entire document will provide additional insight. If you highlight an entire section of text with your cursor, for instance, this information will change from the total number of words to x of x words, which indicates how many words the highlighted section has relative to the entire file.

Following this is an image of a small book containing either a checkmark or a 'x'. This is the indication from the editor. If it has a checkmark, the document contains no errors that need to be corrected. As you might expect, an x signifies that corrections are necessary. You can view the necessary corrections by clicking this book twice at the bottom of the page. However, this is related to the next thing you will see, which is the language used by the program to correct your document. This will appear with the language and country it refers to between parentheses, as the grammar and spelling of some words may vary by country, even among speakers of the same language. To modify this, simply double-click it, and a window will appear from which you can select the desired idiom.

Starting Off

Let's start a new document now that you know what each tool is for. If you're already in Word and want to start a new file, simply **click the File button and select New Document.** This is the same button that you would use to save the document or Save As if you wanted to save it with a different extension, such as.pdf, or with a different name.

If you want to open a previously saved document, you can go to the file tab, where you will see a list of recent documents that have been opened as well as those that have been pinned. You can choose a document from this list or use the Open button on the left-hand toolbar to search your computer for the desired document.

When you open the file tab or the software, you'll notice that the top of the page gives you the option of using a template. These are pre-defined standards that Word will provide to help you create useful documents.

If you want to start one that fits in the list, you could use the models and make only minor changes once the file is open.

USING A TEMPLATE

When you go to the home page, Word will automatically identify the documents you use the most and suggest them to you. **If your desired action is not on the list, you can always click on the far-right link that says More Templates.** The software will then display a list of all the template models it has categorized.

They range from a basic resume and cover letter to party invitation flyers and certificate templates. If you don't want them to be displayed, you can always use the search bar at the top to look for online templates. Even if the option you're looking for, such as a business card model, is available, you can always look for more—the software's online database has several options that it will bring you based on your preferences.

FORMATTING THE TEXT

When you write a document, you can present it in a variety of ways, ranging from the color of the font to the alignment of the text. This can make a significant difference in the presentation of a resume, for example; therefore, it is critical to make all necessary changes before submitting it to someone else. This chapter will teach you how to format text for the best results when defining your document.

How to work with Words

Assume you've started a new document. You may want to specify the type of font, size, and color you want to use here. All of this can be done in the font section's **Home tab**. There are two approaches you can take here: You can type the text, select each section to change, click the buttons, or start from scratch with the formatting. As you can see, there is a small box with an arrow next to the **word font**; by clicking on it, you will gain access to additional font tools for your document.

The advantage of clicking on this button and using the feature is that you will see a preview of what will happen to your text based on your selection.

The user can see the font in the selected text and change the style (bold, italic, or underlined), font size, color, and special effects (superscript, all caps, or strikethrough). Because the majority of these features are also available in the ribbon, either option could be used.

When you open the dialogue box, the advanced text features that are not on the ribbon are displayed in a tab next to the Font.

This section also allows the user to preview how each of the changes will look when applied to the text, similar to how the font tab works. However, you will be able to adjust the spacing between characters, their position, and the style you want to apply to the selected portion of the file here.

If you don't want to use the dialogue box, Word simplifies the letter selection by showing what each of these fonts looks like in the drop-down menu. The same fonts are available in both locations, but using the ribbon is faster and easier. The font size will also be available in a drop-down menu, from which you can choose a size or type the number directly to see how much the text will expand. Other font size options include clicking on the 'A' with an arrow pointing up to increase font size or clicking on the 'A' with an arrow pointing down to decrease font size.

The button with an **uppercase and lowercase 'A'** will determine how your sentence is capitalized. For example, suppose you wrote something in normal sentence case but now want to emphasize it by making it all uppercase. It is not necessary to delete it in order to change it. Simply select the part of the text you want to change, click this button, and then select **UPPERCASE** to make them all capital.

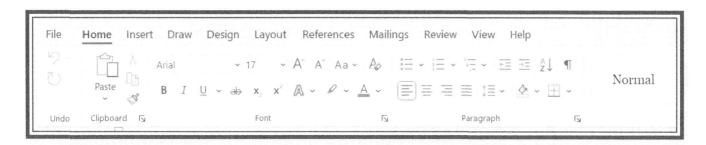

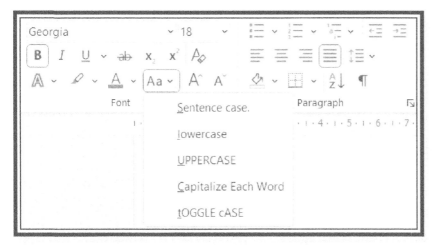

The highlighting function (the 'ABC' with a yellow bar), font color (the 'A' with a red bar), superscript, under script, and strikethrough are also easily accessible.

However, you may have noticed that one button was not mentioned. This is the letter **'A' with a small pink square** next to it—it is one of the most useful tools! It is the format **delete button**. Assume you've formatted a text and don't like it or want to change it. You can clear the formatting and start over by selecting the text you want to change and clicking on this button. This is a more convenient and faster way to undo your actions than pressing the button..

Pro tip: You'll notice a paintbrush in the **ribbon's home tab**. This paintbrush is used to format sections of the document in a manner similar to the one selected. To use it, first select the text from which the style should be copied. Then, you select the paintbrush and navigate to the section of text that you want to format. When you're finished, you'll notice that the text has been formatted in the same way. This saves you from having to manually format all of the document's sections. However, once you've finished making your selection, the paintbrush will be deactivated automatically. If you want to format more than one section this way, click on the paintbrush twice; it will only deactivate when you click on it again.

Paragraph symbol

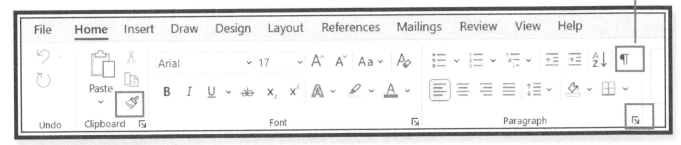

Paintbrush

*Click to open
the Dialog Box*

How to Format Paragraph

The next step is to format the paragraph after you have already formatted the words to your preferences. It is possible to change the default left alignment that Word uses for text.

The **paragraph function**, like the font function, has a box with an arrow next to it that activates a dialogue box with additional options. You can access other tools using the dialogue box even though the buttons on the ribbon are more user-friendly.

This box will allow you to see, at the bottom, what will happen to the selected text depending on the option you select, much like the font function does.

22°C
Sunny

Search

09:00 AM
01/09/202

Pro tip: To control the spacing and visualize how many spaces you have used to separate each paragraph, use the **Paragraph symbol button** on the top right-hand corner of the paragraph section. This is only for visualization and will not be printed in your document or visible if you save it as a PDF.

This is just for visualization purposes while you use the document and can be an asset if you are critical of the formatting of your document. This tool will also enable you to visualize the page breaks you add, the number of tabs placed, and other functions you apply to the file.

For instance, suppose you are **writing a letter** and wish to place the address in the upper right-hand corner. In this situation, you would select the correct option. To center a title, you would use the centered feature, and to align text on both sides, you would use the justified option. The ribbon contains all of the available options, with lines representing what would happen to the text if that option were chosen.

You can also choose to indent the first sentence of a paragraph by clicking the indent button or adjusting the line spacing.

To determine the spacing between the lines, you must click the button with one arrow pointing up and one arrow pointing down.

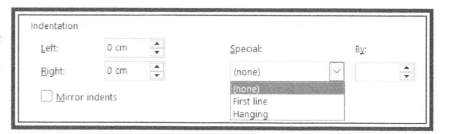

From there, you can choose whether you want a simple 1 pixel space, 1.5 pixels, and so on. You will click line spacing options to customize the distance between lines of text or to add a single space before or after a paragraph.

This is particularly useful for authors of scientific articles, theses, and other documents requiring a particular format. If your document will be uniform throughout, you can click the set as default button in the dialogue box to apply this setting to the entire document. To make it even simpler, after clicking it, you will be asked if you want to define this style only for this document or for all files based on the default template. In this instance, it is up to you to determine your preference.

This section also provides the option to generate lists using bullet points or numbers. On the ribbon, these are denoted by numbers or squares followed by lines. The good news is that you can choose the format for these as well. By clicking on the arrow next to these boxes, you will be able to choose the type of bullet point marker or the format for your numbered list's numbers and letters. The multilevel list is an additional feature that is available.

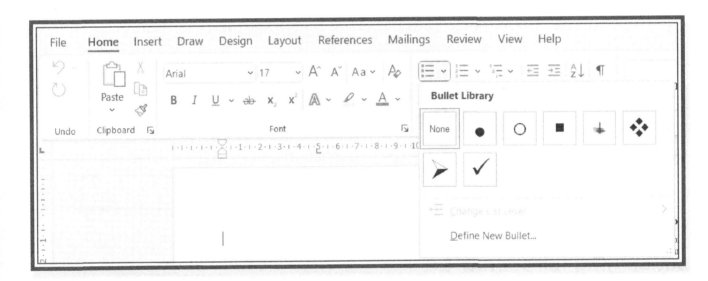

Pro tip: If you're using a numbered list or a bulleted list, write one sentence using it and hit **enter on the following line to automatically add a new bullet point** or number to the list. You have to press backspace and wait until the next sentence's margin to delete it. You have two choices if you want to keep going with the list: either keep writing and hit enter so that the bullet points are generated automatically, or make a list with levels. Simply click the tab before you begin writing to create a list with levels. The bullet point or number will then move and be automatically updated to the new format.

22°C Sunny 🔍 Search W X P A O S T N P 09:00 AM 01/09/202

Organize a list in alphabetical order

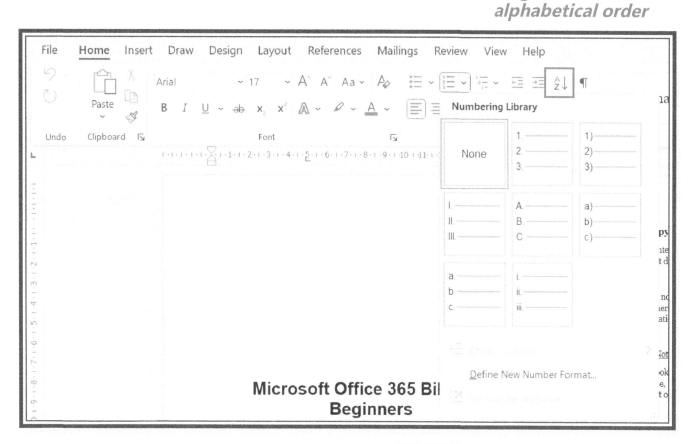

A list can be arranged alphabetically by selecting it and selecting the button with the letters "AZ" and an arrow pointing down in the paragraph formatting. By selecting the square button on this section of the ribbon, you can also decide to surround the text or lines with a box on either side, above, or below.

Use the **paint bucket** to choose the color you want, and it will be filled in automatically, to add color to the paragraph, section, or line.

Last but not least, imagine that you are writing a news article that calls for the use of columns. Did you know Word has a feature for that as well? Simply choose the text you want to convert to this format, navigate to the layout tab, and click the columns button.

The user can choose how many columns to separate the text into in this basic setting. The arrow at the end of the list will open a dialogue box that will help you decide (and visualize) the width of the columns, whether you want a line to separate them, and where you want to apply the configuration, but if you want more information on how it is formatted.

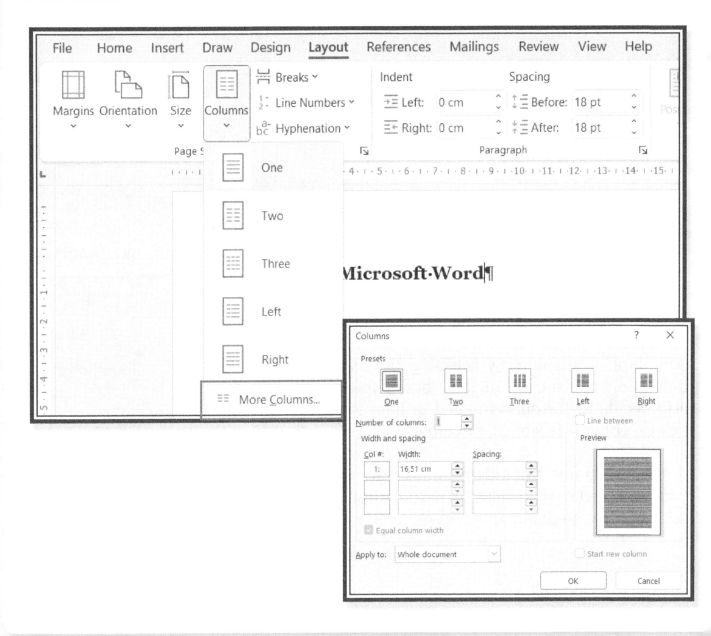

VIEWING AND FORMATTING THE DOCUMENT

It's time to make changes to your document after the text has been formatted. Word offers the user a number of features to customize the document however they want. Once more, those who must write in a specific format or who are subject to strict requirements regarding the appearance of the document may find these tools to be of particular benefit. Continue reading to learn how to define the parameters for your file and customize it to your specifications.

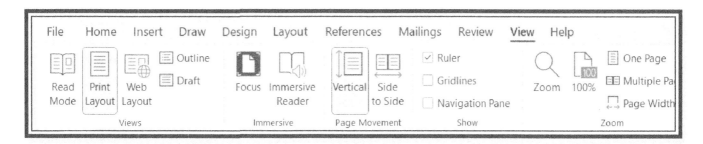

Pro tip: *Choose the print layout view from the view tab of your ribbon to better see the document changes and settings.* **This will give you a clearer idea of how the file appears and make it simpler for you to picture changes.** *The read mode and draft view are two additional options in this view. To make reading easier, the* **read mode** *fills the entire screen and hides the toolbars, and the* **draft view** *hides the content margins. The most comprehensive view for those who want to see how their document will appear once it is finished is the print layout view.*

Margins and Page Settings

The first thing you can do is choose whether the page will be **landscape or portrait** to specify the configuration of the page. To do this, click the down-pointing arrow on the **orientation** button while in the layout tab of the ribbon, then choose the one you want to use.

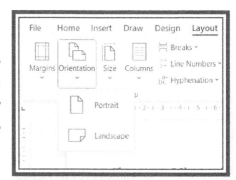

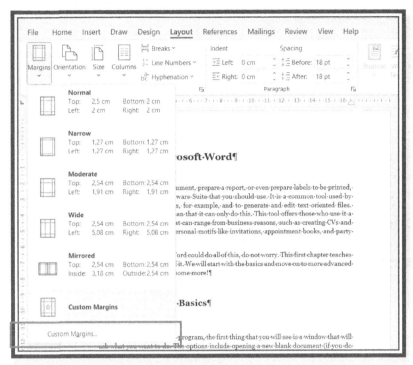

The layout of the page will change immediately as a result of this relatively easy change.

The margins that you want the document to have can then be customized. While you're still in the ribbon area, click the **margins button** and choose from the pre-built formats or **customize** them as you like. A dialogue box will open when you click the customize margins button at the bottom of the list, allowing you to enter the measurements as needed.

Pro tip: *You can always use the ruler to manually see or move the margins for yourself. Go to the view tab, where you can check the box labeled "ruler" to make the ruler appear or disappear. The ruler will appear in your document window (but won't print or be saved) if it is checked; if it is not, it will vanish. Use the double arrows on the ruler to reposition your document's margins and paragraph indents. Move the gray areas of the ruler to choose the margin size you want to manually change. .*

Ruler

Additionally, you can decide whether your document will have a book fold using this dialogue box, saving you from having to configure it further, and you can choose the paper size you want to use. The user can select the paper size from a list or enter custom measurements for the **paper's width and height by selecting the paper tab** on the second tab of this dialogue box. The user can decide whether the style they chose will be the default for both the document and all new files, just like it was in the font section.

Let's say you've finished writing a section and want to begin a new section on the following page. The enter key doesn't need to be depressed until you get to it. The document can have page breaks, which will take you directly to the next page.

To use this tool, navigate to the insert tab of your ribbon. There, under the pages section, you'll find the options to **add a cover page** (you can choose from a number of different styles), and a break will be placed automatically to allow you to add a blank page to the document at any time.

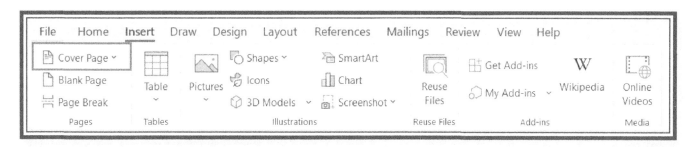

Cover Page options

Another option is to merely insert a page break. You will automatically add a page after the one where your cursor is if you click the **page break button.** However, it is also possible to create a page break and carry on writing on the same page.

To do this, select the arrow from the breaks button in the page setup section of the layout tab. Here, the user can specify whether they want a page break that goes to the following page, a column break, or a text-wrapping break. (See the image in the next page.)

If what you want to do is define a section, you will need to decide whether to move the text to the following page, keep it on the current page, or move it to an even or an odd-numbered page.

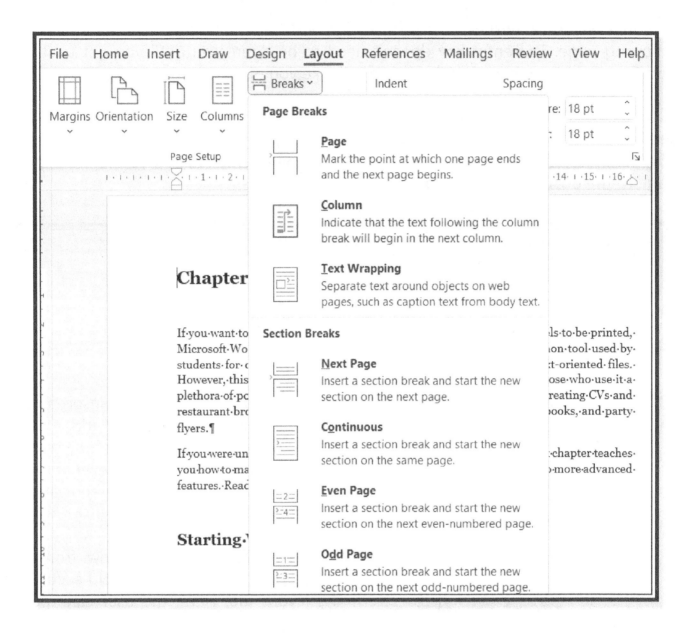

It's time to delve a little deeper now that you have seen some of Word's fundamental features and how to operate some of its key tools. Next, we'll look at some of the extra features and functions that can be added to your document to give it more value. Let's look at how we can use tables to get things going.

MAKING AND UTILIZING TABLES

When writing a document, we occasionally feel the need to better organize our content. To do this, we need to make a table. This is incredibly simple to do in Word documents. The tool allows you to choose the number of rows and columns as well as whether or not to combine any of the resources.

You must select the **insert tab** and look for the second section, which is labeled "table," in order to insert a table. You can choose the squares that represent the number of fields for each row or column by clicking on the arrow that points down. The configuration you have chosen is displayed at the top of the drop-down menu as you make your selection.

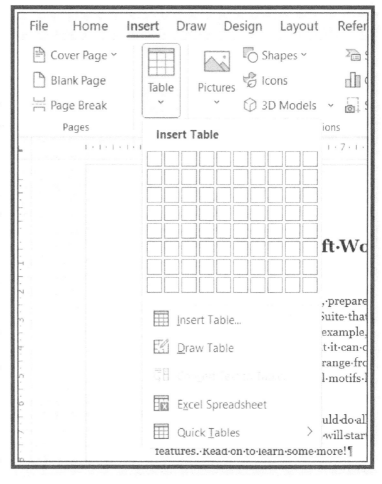

If you'd prefer to choose the number of columns and rows manually, you can click the **insert table button**. This will bring up a dialogue box where you can enter the desired number of columns and rows, the width of each column (which is predetermined as fixed), and whether you want the table to automatically fit the page. You can decide right here if this is the standard you want for upcoming tables.

Additionally, you can draw the table yourself using this menu and add a really useful feature by including an Excel spreadsheet in your document. Making use of all the features of the spreadsheet will make it simpler to add calculations without running the risk of making a mistake.

As you'll see in the section below, you can also create graphs and charts to include in your document. For more details on using Excel, please refer to Chapter 2.

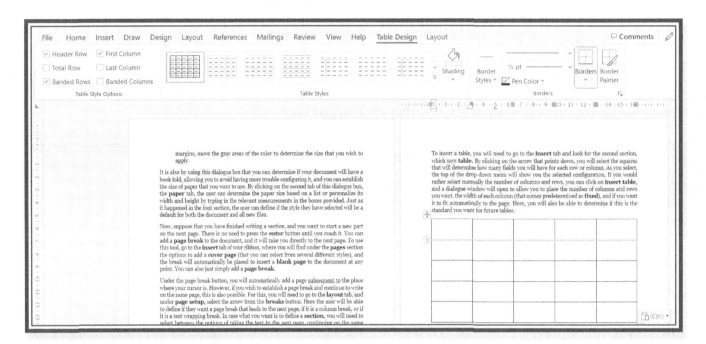

> **Pro tip:** After inserting a table, a new tab titled **"table tools"** will be added to the top menu. You can choose the table layout and design here, as well as the style of the line, whether you want to add or remove rows, whether you want to add a specific style, how to sort the columns alphabetically, how to color a particular cell, and how to merge or split cells. Keep in mind that all the other aspects of the text you have already learned still apply!

CREATE GRAPHS AND FORMULAS

Imagine you are creating a business report that needs to include graphs and statistics. In that case, you can include these in your document using Word. The option to add illustrations, including graphs, can be found by selecting the **"insert" tab**. There is no need to be concerned if the data is not in an Excel spreadsheet. A dialogue box will open after you click the button to add a chart, allowing you to select the type. In the preferences, you can choose from histograms, pie charts, and column charts.

22°C Sunny   Search   09:00 AM 01/09/202...

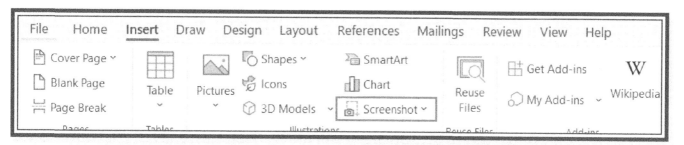

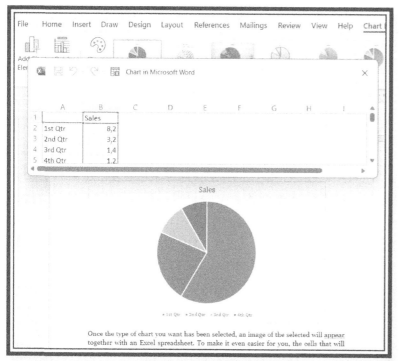

Once the desired chart type has been chosen, an image of the choice and an Excel spreadsheet will both appear.

The cells that will hold the information will already be visible, naming everything that needs to be entered into each box to produce the desired image, making it even simpler for you.

Using your knowledge, fill in the labels and series as necessary. But this spreadsheet won't show up in your document.

Your chart should automatically update once you have finished entering the data; you will then need to click the x button to close it. Your modifications won't be ignored.

22°C Sunny
Search

> *Pro tip:* Click **Edit Data** to make changes to the information in the Excel spreadsheet. If the data for the table you want to create is already present in another file, you can choose where it will come from by clicking on Select Data. This will launch a dialogue box to look for the file on your computer.

As an added bonus, the Chart tools tab will always open whenever you want to work with the chart, just like with the table feature. The user can add chart elements, modify the layout, and even choose the style they want to be used by clicking on it. Additionally, you can pick the colors for the bars. You can make these adjustments manually in the Format tab of the chart tools if you don't want to use any of the predefined styles.

Chart Design tab

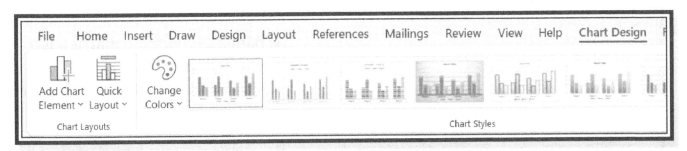

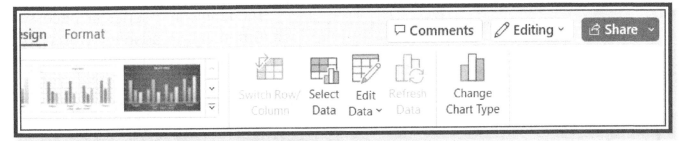

You can resize your chart by dragging one of the image's tips, where a circle is present, up or down, or you can enter the size in the height and width boxes on the ribbon. Imagine that you want the text and the image of this graph or chart to be aligned so that the image is on one side and the text is on the other. Then, you must use the **wrap text** function to accomplish this. The **arrange tab** will open up a number of options when you click on the downward-pointing icon, each with a visual representation of where you want the image to be placed.

22°C
Sunny
Search

09:00 AM
01/09/202

PICTURES, SHAPES, AND SMARTART

Images shouldn't pose too much of a challenge for you if you are already an expert at using graphs and charts and formatting them within your document. You will notice that there are connections between each of the categories mentioned in this section, despite the fact that each is a world unto itself. When writing a document that requires visual aids to help the reader better understand your point, all of these components will be useful. Let's start by discussing images.

Pictures

Although you can **insert a picture** using the keyboard shortcut (see shortcut keys at the end of this chapter). You can also do so by using the ribbon.

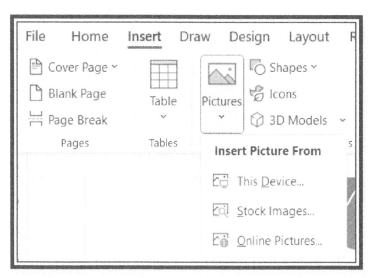

You can add a picture from your computer or an online source by selecting the "insert" tab. Your preference and whether the desired image is already on your device will determine how you proceed.

After you've added the image, a brand-new toolbar for picture settings will show up on the ribbon. Use the corrections button in the adjust section if your selected image needs any adjustments. You can edit the photo or make any other necessary changes using this section of the ribbon. Additionally, if there is something you want to undo, you have the option of resetting it.

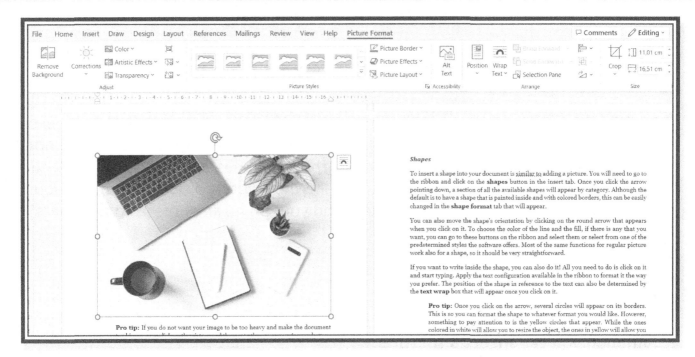

Pro tip: *You can click on the image and then select the **compress image button** if you don't want your image to be too large and expand the document. Here, you can select the resolution you want and decide whether you want the compression applied only to these images or to all of the images in the document (click or unclick on the box). Word will provide a brief explanation of each resolution so you can choose more intelligently which one to use.*

Manually adjusting the image is yet another option. You can do this by dragging it or moving it to the desired size in the box. You will also be able to crop the image in this section. The ability to rotate the image, choose its location, and specify the placement of the text next to it are additional features.

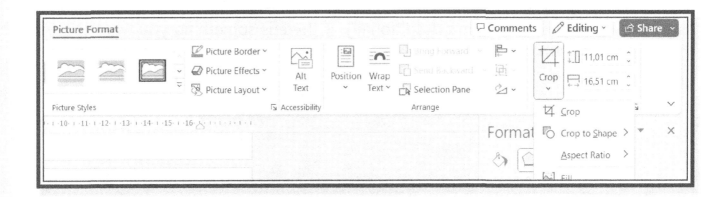

Pro tip: Since most of us have limited control over how to maintain the width and length of the image, it often happens that when we manually adjust the **picture size**, it becomes distorted. All you need to do when manually moving the image is keep the **shift button** depressed to preserve the proportions of the original image. By maintaining the ratio between length and width and preventing distortion, this will allow the image to retain its original qualities.

Shapes

It's similar to adding a picture to your document to **insert a shape.** You must access the ribbon and select the insert tab's shapes button. A section of all the available shapes will show up by category once you click the arrow pointing down.

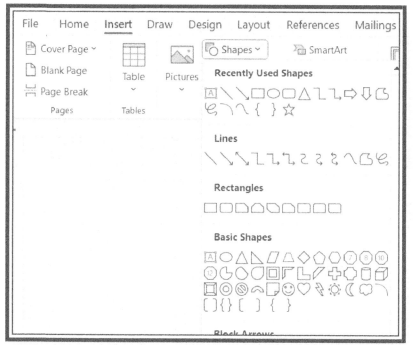

The **shape format tab** that will appear allows you to easily change the default shape, which has a painted interior and colored borders.

By clicking on the circular arrow that appears when you click on the shape, you can also change the orientation of the object.

You can go to these buttons on the ribbon and select the line and fill colors, if you so desire, or you can choose from one of the predetermined styles the software provides. Since a shape can perform most of the same operations as a regular picture, it should be very simple.

File Home Insert Draw Design Layout References Mailings Review View Help **Shape Format**

Shapes

To insert a shape into your document is similar to adding a picture. You will need to go to the ribbon and click on the **shapes** button in the insert tab. Once you click the arrow pointing down, a section of all the available shapes will appear by category. Although the default is to have a shape that is painted inside and with colored borders, this can be easily changed in the **shape format** tab that will appear.

If you want to write inside the shape, you can also do that! You only need to click it and begin typing. Use the text formatting options in the ribbon to format it how you like. The text wrap box that will appear once you click on it will also show you where the shape should be placed in relation to the text.

Pro tip: A number of circles will start to appear on the arrow's borders once you click it. This enables you to format the shape in any way that you choose. However, the yellow circles that appear are something to be aware of. The objects that are highlighted in white can be resized, whereas the objects that are highlighted in yellow can have their format changed. Two yellow circles, one at the start and one at the head of the arrow, will show up, for instance, if you use the arrow shape. While the rest of the arrow stays the same, if you move the one at the head, you can choose whether you want it to be narrower or wider. Use the same method of pressing the shift button for resizing problems.

SmartArt

Making the document simpler to work with is the one thing Word can do to benefit the user. You can add processes, hierarchies, pyramids, and cycle images using the **SmartArt feature**. As with the previous two items, go to the insert tab on the ribbon to add one of these based on your needs. When you choose SmartArt, a dialogue box with options will appear for you to select from. You should select the option here that best fits your project.

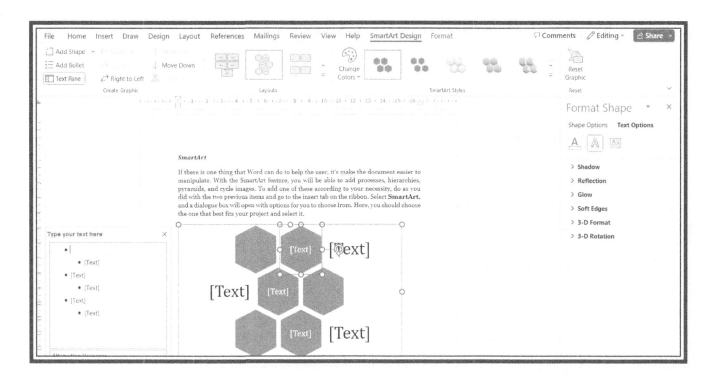

Once you've selected the option that works best for your file, it will show up already colored and with options for where to add text. The additional features are offered by a **SmartArt tab** that will appear on the ribbon, and the user can choose what to write in this area. You will be able to alter the structure's colors, move it around, and add new shapes. As usual, the text must be specified in the Font toolbar.

> *Pro tip:* Let's say you want to expand the structure you just made with a form. Choose with your cursor which of the boxes (or forms) you want the extra element to be added to so that it isn't added at the end. It will be added at the end if you simply leave the structure clicked without choosing a specific shape. The shape will automatically be added after the selected element if you choose add shape while selecting a specific element in the middle of the format, saving you the time and effort of having to redo the entire format.

CREATING A TABLE OF CONTENTS AND REFERENCES

One of Word's best features is the ability to format a table of contents and add references automatically without the need for any manual work. You can automatically create and format your document with just a few clicks and a few formatting pointers. Can you believe it even does your bibliography preparation for you? You will spend much less time writing down your sources if you do this. Let's look at it!

Table of Contents

A table of contents is simpler to make than you might imagine. The **Styles** section of the ribbon under the **Home tab** is the first thing you should keep in mind. Let's say you want to write a technical book with a number of chapter headings and subtitles. If so, **Heading 1** would be the title of the chapter, **Heading 2** the subtitle of the chapter's sections, **Heading 3** the section below that, and so on. You will select and click each of the headings that you feel are appropriate for your section as you create the sections and titles for your chapters and sections.

22°C Sunny · Search · 09:00 AM 01/09/202.

You should continue doing this until every page of the book has a style assigned. You can check the format feature to see if each section title has a small square and an arrow next to it to make sure the style has been applied. You will be able to tell if they have been applied correctly thanks to this. For your convenience, Word will let you rename each heading structure in accordance with what it will represent in your file. It can be changed to a section, chapter, subtitle, or anything else you deem fit.

Pro tip: You can modify the style of each of these headings! Simply place your right mouse or touchpad button on top of it to bring up a dialogue box where you can select Modify and make the desired changes.

Another method is to format the text by hand in the document. To do this, select the text you want to change, click on the style to bring up a dialogue box, and then choose **Update Heading x to match selection.** This will automatically change the style of all of your headings of that type.

You must navigate to the reference tab in the ribbon after formatting the file and adding the desired headings. The **Table of Contents** button is located in the bottom left corner. Select the option you want to use for your document by clicking the button and choosing it from the drop-down menu. It will all be automatically displayed with the headings you chose. Please leave room in your document for the table of contents, if applicable.

You can work with the document normally after the table of contents appears without having to worry about updating it. If you choose, you can click on it to bring up an update option with a red exclamation point. The ribbon also has this choice available. Use the font-change buttons on the ribbon to format the table of contents font.

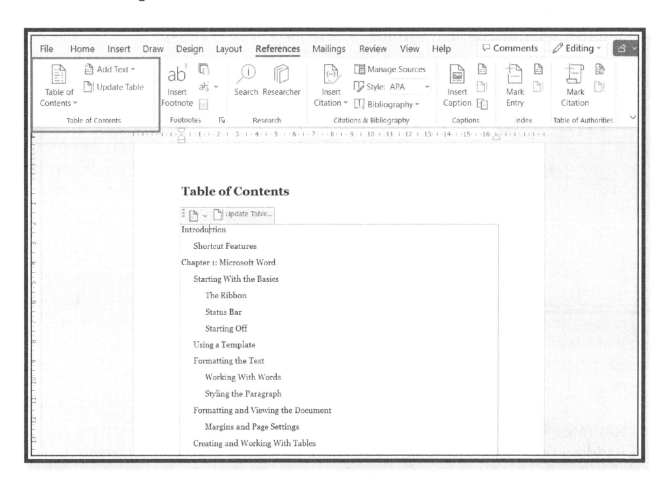

Inserting Footnotes

There may be times when adding footnotes as references is part of the writing process. Word will let you add them and number them for you automatically. When the cursor is placed next to the word that the footnote will refer to, select **Insert Footnote** from the reference tab. The document will take you to the end of the page, where you can type in what you need, and a small superscript number will automatically appear next to the text.

If you need to include a footnote somewhere in the document, do not be concerned.

The numbers and the order will be updated for you automatically by the software. In accordance with the location of the reference word, it will also move the footnote to the appropriate page.

Simply click the Next footnote button on the ribbon **to jump to the next footnote** in the document if you want to browse through all of them.

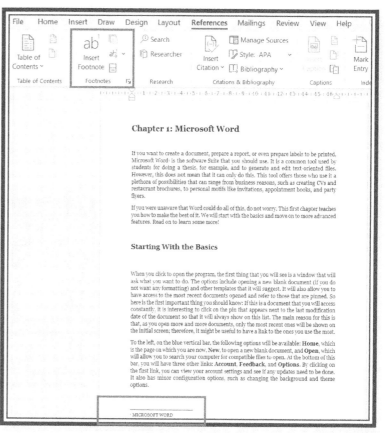

Footnote

How to Insert Captions

For the images you are applying, you might also need to add captions. Word has a feature for this as well. You must choose the photo or image you want to use as a reference before clicking the **Insert caption button** on the ribbon. When you do, a dialogue box will appear where you can name it and select whether you want it to be displayed as a figure, equation, or table. The correct information must be entered because doing so will later allow you to insert a table of figures into your document.

With this feature, you can either use the chapter numbers or a straightforward chronological order to number the figures. Everything will be done based on your preferences. When you're finished, choose where you want the table of figures to be created and press the corresponding button to have it done for you. When you are still in the draft stage of the file, there is not much need to worry about the order or page numbers being correct because you will be able to update it automatically just like the table of contents.

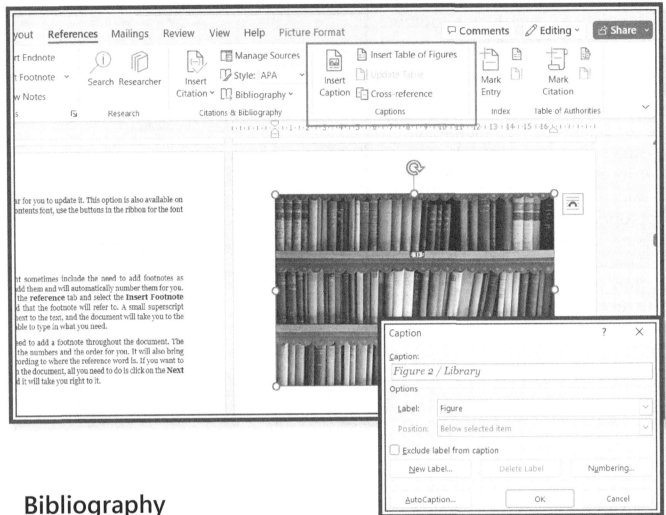

ut **References** Mailings Review View Help Picture Format 💬 Comments ✎ Editing ⌄ 🖼 Share ⌄

rt Endnote
Footnote ⌄   Search Researcher   Insert Citation ⌄   ☐ Manage Sources   Insert Caption   📄 Insert Table of Figures   Mark Entry   Mark Citation
w Notes   ☐ Style: APA   ☐ Update Table
                                                      ☐ Bibliography ⌄   ☐ Cross-reference

s   Research   Citations & Bibliography   Captions   Index   Table of Authorities

r for you to update it. This option is also available on
ntents font, use the buttons in the ribbon for the font

t sometimes include the need to add footnotes as
dd them and will automatically number them for you.
the **reference** tab and select the **Insert Footnote**
d that the footnote will refer to. A small superscript
ext to the text, and the document will take you to the
ble to type in what you need.

eed to add a footnote throughout the document. The
the numbers and the order for you. It will also bring
ording to where the reference word is. If you want to
h the document, all you need to do is click on the **Next**
d it will take you right to it.

Caption   ?   ✕

Caption:

Figure 2 / Library

Options

Label: Figure   ⌄

Position: Below selected item   ⌄

☐ Exclude label from caption

New Label...   Delete Label   Numbering...

AutoCaption...   OK   Cancel

Bibliography

If it's not your habit, making a bibliography can be time-consuming and difficult. As a result, Word will make your work easier by performing it for you as you enter the data.

The format you want to use—APA, Vancouver, ISO, or another—must be chosen first. Once this is configured, you can click the **Insert Citation** button to add the necessary information. A dialogue box will then open.

Insert Citation ⌄   ☐ Manage Sources   ☐ Style: APA ⌄   Insert   📄 Insert Ta
☐ Biblio   ☐ Update

Citations & Biblio

APA
Sixth Edition

Chicago
Sixteenth Edition

GB7714
2005

GOST - Name Sort
2003

GOST - Title Sort
2003

Once you've finished entering all the necessary information, simply click the **Bibliography button,** and a reference section will be generated for you based on the style you've chosen.

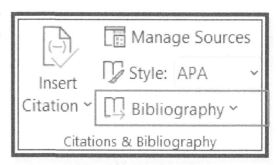

REVIEW, TRANSLATION, AND SPELL CHECK.

If you want to present a credible document that is error-free, you must use the spell check feature. By selecting your preferred language from the **status bar** at the bottom or by going to the **review tab** on the ribbon, Word will let you proofread the document in that language. Additionally, you can select a specific section of the document and use the appropriate language to only spell check that section.

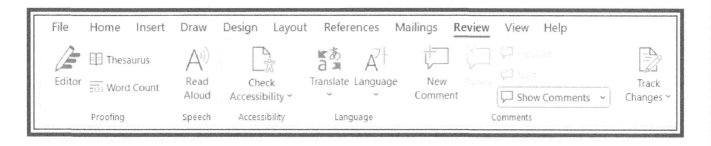

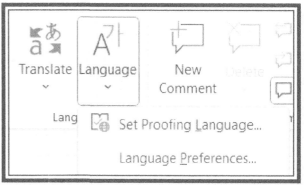

However, you will use the software's online features if your goal is to translate a particular passage. You can choose to translate the entire document, a specific section, or just a single word while editing the document.

A mini translation will appear if you keep the mouse arrow over the word. Depending on your goals for the document, this will vary. After translating the document, you can use spell check to make sure everything is accurate.

Finally, but certainly not least, imagine that you are currently editing a document for a friend and want them to see the changes you made. Although it is not required, some people choose to highlight these in the file. By choosing the **Tracking option**, you can **keep track of all the changes that have been made** and decide whether or not to **accept or reject them.** Depending on your preference, you can complete these one at a time or all at once. Use the Compare function to see all the changes made to the original file if the reviewer did not track changes for you to see.

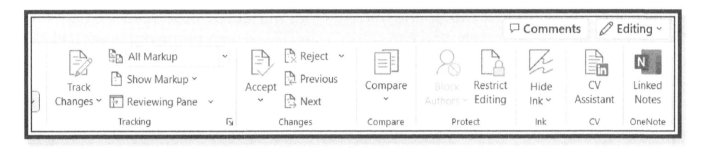

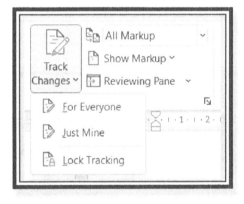

22°C
Sunny

O Search

09:00 AM
01/09/202

KEYBOARD SHORTCUTS

FUNCTION	SHORTCUT ON PC	SHORTCUT ON MAC
Start a new document	Ctrl + N	Command + N
Open a new document	Ctrl + O	Command + O
Save the document	Ctrl + S	Command + S
Cut content	Ctrl + X	Command + X or F2
Paste content	Ctrl + V	Command + V or F4
Copy content	Ctrl + C	Command + C or F3
Make font bold	Ctrl + B	Command + B
Underline selection	Ctrl + U	Command + U
Make font italic	Ctrl + I	Command + I
Undo previous action	Ctrl + Z	Command + Z or F1
Print	Ctrl + P	Command + P
Move cursor to top	Ctrl + Alt + Page Up	Command + Page Up
Move cursor down	Ctrl + Alt + Page Down	Command + Page Down
Select whole document	Ctrl + A	Command + A
Insert page break	Ctrl + Enter	Command + Return
Insert line break	Shift + Enter	Shift + Return
Insert column break	Ctrl + Shift + Enter	Command + Shift + Return
Insert copyright symbol	Ctrl + Alt + C	Not available
Insert trademark symbol	Ctrl + Alt + T	Option + 2

Section 2:
Microsoft EXCEL

Microsoft Excel is a software application that forms an integral component of the Office Suite. It is primarily employed for performing calculations, generating reports, and facilitating the organization of financial data. In addition to facilitating the utilization of formulas for intricate computations, the software offers a plethora of supplementary functionalities, including the creation of forms, incorporation of graphical representations, and the ability to conduct data analysis. While the topic of Excel's versatility in program creation is beyond the scope of this book, it is noteworthy to acknowledge that certain individuals employ Excel for this purpose.

Prior to delving into the specific details of the program, it is important to take note of a small disclaimer. The ribbon interface across the majority of Office applications exhibits uniformity, thus obviating the need for a comprehensive examination of its constituent elements in subsequent chapters. Given that the majority of features exhibit uniformity and share identical commands, including the utilization of equivalent shortcut keys, the forthcoming chapters will concentrate on the distinctive tools.

This approach aims to enhance the reading experience by offering supplementary insights and facilitating the acquisition of novel functionalities inherent to each individual

22°C
Sunny

Search

09:00 AM
01/09/2023

program. If there are any features that you require assistance with, please consult Chapter 1 for further clarification. Are you prepared to acquire a comprehensive understanding of the essential functionalities of this remarkable software?

LET'S START WITH THE BASICS

Upon launching Excel for the initial time and creating a new file, users will observe the appearance of a document comprising grids, commonly referred to as spreadsheets.

These spreadsheets serve as the fundamental structure within the software that users will employ for various purposes. By default, Microsoft Excel will open a single worksheet, representing the project on which you will be working.

In the event that your project necessitates division into multiple interconnected spreadsheets, it is possible to generate several worksheets by selecting the '+' button adjacent to the sheet information, as opposed to generating separate files for each individual spreadsheet. Excel provides the capability to incorporate a substantial quantity of interconnected elements.

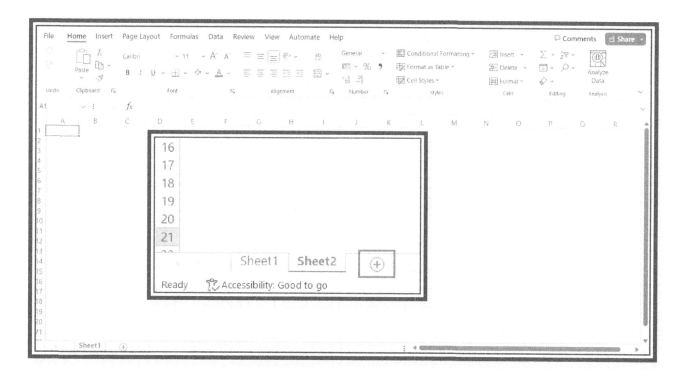

Pro tip: A useful strategy for enhancing control over the contents of individual sheets involves personalizing their names and tab colors. To modify the name of a worksheet, the user can simply double-click on the existing name, typically denoted as **Worksheet 1**, and proceed to enter the desired name.

To arrange the tabs based on their color, users can achieve this by right-clicking on the tab name and selecting the **"Tab Color"** option. In addition to its primary function, the right button also provides several additional options, including the ability to move, protect, or hide the current sheet. Nevertheless, caution should be exercised when considering the deletion of either one of them. Once this action is completed, it becomes irretrievable.

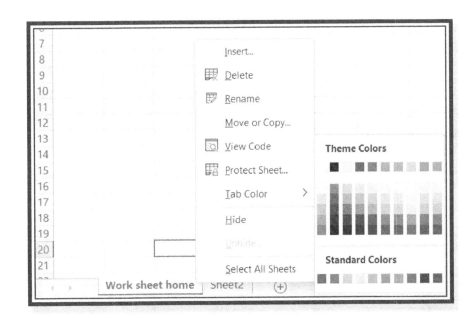

The spreadsheet is partitioned into columns denoted by letters and rows denoted by numbers. It is crucial to bear in mind this information when employing formulas, as they will be expounded upon in subsequent sections of the chapter. In order to adjust the dimensions of a column or row, it is necessary to position the mouse cursor directly above the line associated with the numerical or alphabetical identifier that follows the specific element requiring resizing. Subsequently, a double arrow symbol will become visible. By adjusting its position horizontally or vertically, you can ascertain the desired size.

> ***Pro tip:*** *A useful technique is to resize the cell containing content in order to accommodate the written text within a single line, thereby eliminating the need for manual adjustment of the column. To achieve the desired outcome, simply perform a double-click action on any location within the column line. This action will trigger an automatic adjustment process, wherein the column will adapt its width to accommodate the content with the greatest length.*

We will now move on to the other unique features of the program since the formatting tools for these rows and columns are comparable to those you have used in Word.

SET LAYOUT AND VISUALIZATION

You can view the spreadsheet you are working on using **Excel's layout and visualization features**, which will also help you use some of the program's secret features more effectively.

The **working, reading, and print layout views** are all visible in the bottom right corner of the document, just like in Word. The working view is fairly concise, so we'll move on to examine the features offered by the other visualization options since they are more comprehensive.

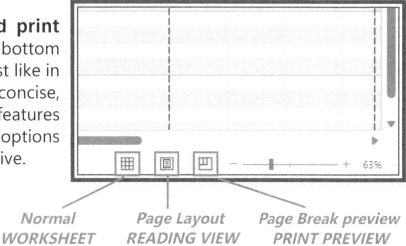

Normal   *Page Layout*   *Page Break preview*
WORKSHEET   *READING VIEW*   *PRINT PREVIEW*

Reading View Mode

This view of the file you are currently editing will allow you to both work with it and view the document's header and footer, allowing you to edit their appearance if the file is saved as.pdf or printed. As with similar views, you can move and resize this view. Using the page **layout tab,** you can view the document in **portrait or landscape mode**, as well as the margins and page breaks that will be applied.

To edit the header and footer of the spreadsheet, you will only need to click on it once. Each will be divided into three sections that will remain constant regardless of the number of columns you have. Excel provides this feature to better organize the document. When you click on either of these, a tab for header and footer will appear on the ribbon, allowing you to add the page number, the current time, and the sheet name, which will all be printed on every page of the document.

Reading View

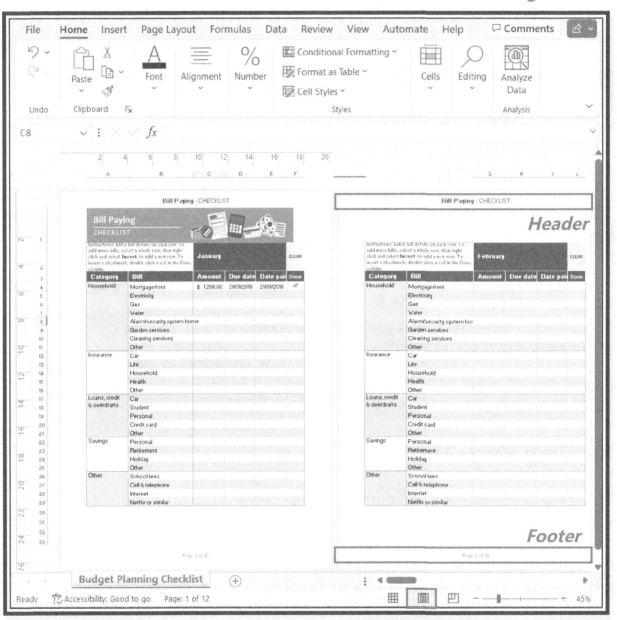

Pro tip: *You cannot add an image to the header or footer in Excel by using the keyboard shortcuts Ctrl (or Command) C and Ctrl (or Command) V. To insert an image in either of these locations, you must use the **Picture tool** on the ribbon. It is also important to note that you will be unable to manually resize it. The user will need to resize the image by trial and error using the **Format Picture toolbox**, which will be accessible after clicking the &[Picture] field.*

Print Preview Mode

Print Preview

The **print preview** option is useful for determining which worksheet sections should be printed. If there is content on your table, it will all be surrounded by blue lines indicating what will be printed if you choose to do so. If there is no content, however, the screen will appear gray. You must move the blue lines to determine what will be printed or saved as a PDF. After it has been calculated automatically based on the margins, you will be able to do so manually in this document.

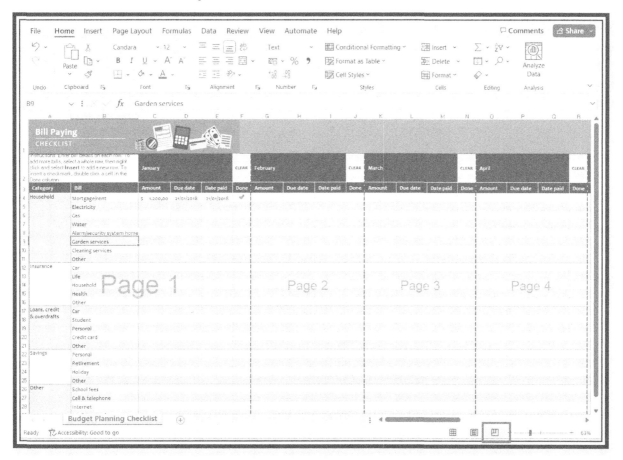

This will allow you to, for example, **adjust the content to fit on one page or divide the content across multiple pages.** The program's recommendation will be represented by a blue dashed line that can be repositioned. To confirm the configuration you've set, simulate printing from the home tab.

Remember that anything outside the blue lines will not be printed or saved.

Pro tip: If you use multiple worksheets, you can configure each one individually and then print them all at once. To print worksheets, you must press the *Ctrl or Command key on your keyboard* and then click on the worksheet's name. Once you navigate to the print view on the File tab, they will all be displayed in the print option. To cancel the selection, move the mouse to one of the worksheet names and click on it; the selection will be removed automatically.

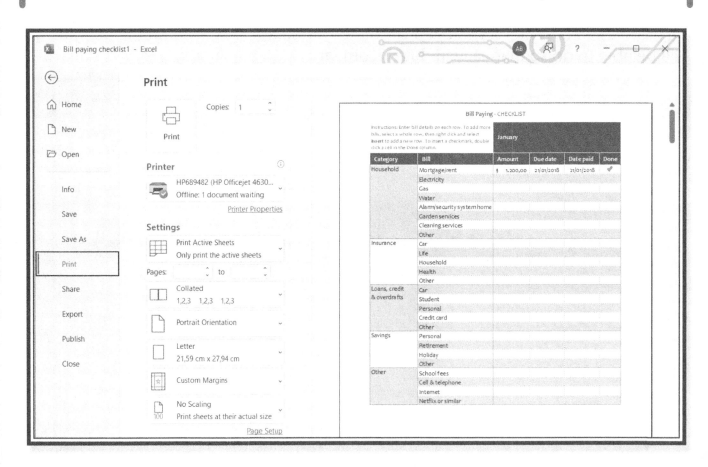

FORMATTING CELLS

One of the most important Excel skills to have is the ability to format cells so that they work for you. You have already seen in Chapter 1 how to change the cell's format and color, so we will proceed directly to the program's specifics.

Home Tab

Style and Numbers

There is a section titled number on the home tab. There will be a drop-down menu for quick formatting, or you can click the arrow in the section's upper right-hand corner to open the dialogue box. We recommend beginning in this manner so that you can visualize your options. Remember that the cell must be selected in order to be formatted. Depending on your needs, you can format a single cell or multiple cells simultaneously.

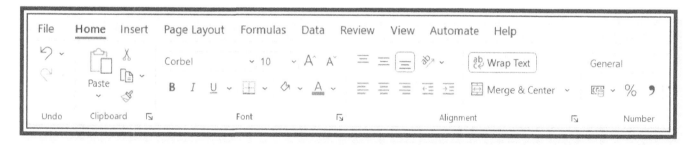

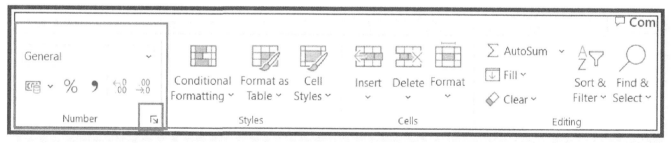

Number section

After opening the dialogue box, you will be able to choose the format for the cell's contents. This is significant because it will have a direct impact on the calculations you perform.

You can select from various formats, including a time format and a custom one. In order to become more familiar with the program, it is suggested that you explore each of them. In addition to alignment, font, border, and fill, this menu also provides options for cell protection and cell protection.

Pro tip: *If you intend to share your spreadsheet with others but do not want them to modify a specific cell or group of cells, you can **lock the cell.** As soon as you select this option on the **Protection tab** of the dialogue box, the program will recognize that this cell requires protection. To complete the process, go to the **review tab** and select the **protect sheet option**. A new dialogue box will appear where you can select the data you wish to lock, and a **password** will be required if the user attempts to modify the locked data.*

Dialog Box >Protection Tab

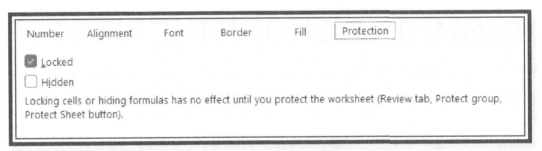

Review Tab

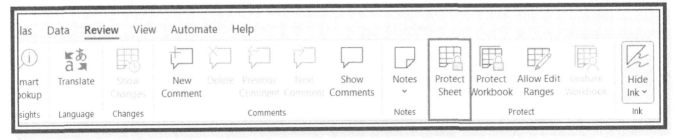

22°C
Sunny   Search

09:00 AM
01/09/202

How to set Conditional Formatting?

This is one of the most useful functions once you begin performing calculations. It will enable Excel to automatically format cells containing a specific value.

Click the **conditional formatting** button on the home tab and select a new rule to use it. A dialogue box will appear, allowing you to select what you wish to format, such as the option to format cells containing specific attributes.

Suppose you select the following option: You will be able to set the rule for your entire worksheet or for selected cells, rows, or columns.

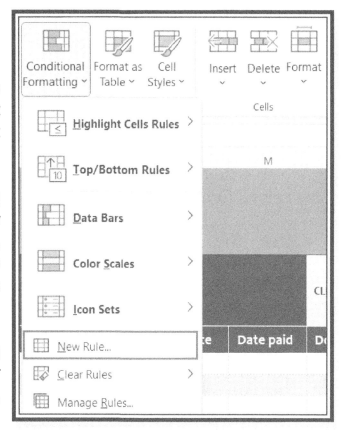

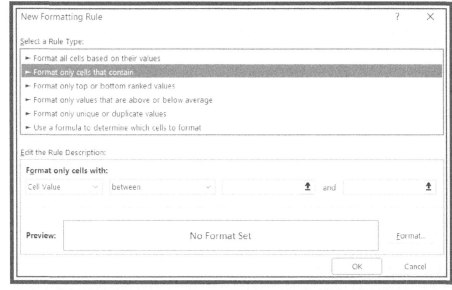

Once you've set the rules based on the assistant, you can click the format button to customize the appearance of these cells.

Remember to select the cells to which this will be applied prior to doing so.

If you want to delete certain rules or view which ones are currently being used in the spreadsheet, you can return to the conditional formatting button and select the appropriate options. In addition to color scales, icons, data bars, and ranking, you can also apply conditional formatting to your worksheet by using color scales, icons, and rankings.

All of these are accessible via the function's drop-down menu and have assistants to help you choose which style to apply.

Other Formatting Tips and Tricks

Once you have mastered cell management, everything else will become simpler. Here are some helpful formatting suggestions:

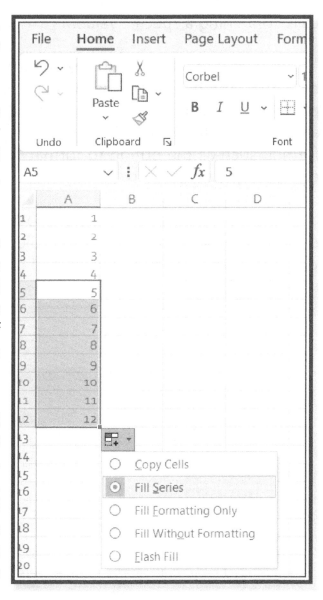

- **Use the paintbrush:** Utilize the paintbrush tool to format all of your cells in the desired style. If you need more information on how to use it, please refer to *Chapter 1, Formatting.*

- **Series or repetition**: If you want to copy the same content to the next line or row, you do not need to copy and paste it manually. When you move the mouse to the bottom-right corner of the cell containing the original text, a cross symbol will appear.

   Click on it with the mouse and drag until you reach the desired location for the series or repetition to continue, and the system will do it automatically. Once you are finished, a small box will appear next to it, from which you can select the desired action, such as filling in the series or simply repeating the formatting.

- **Moving a cell:** You can also relocate a cell from its initial position. In this instance, instead of bringing the mouse to the bottom right corner, you select the cell and then click on any of its lines. The screen will display a cross with four arrows. Then,

you should click on it with the mouse and drag it to the desired location. The formatting will accompany it.

Pro tip: *When moving or duplicating cells, keep in mind that any formatting or formulas will remain intact. Nevertheless, if your cell is part of a formula, this may alter the results, and you may need to modify the information in the row and column where the calculation is being performed.*

Home Tab

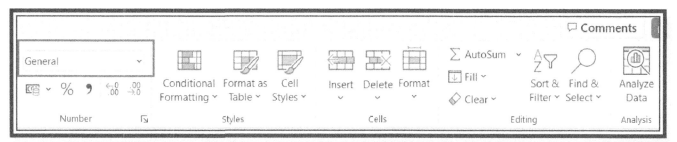

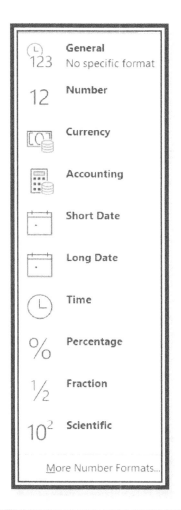

- **Date formatting:** Date formatting advice is the most perplexing of all the guidelines. **If your cell is not set to either the general or date format, a number will appear when you enter data.** This is due to the fact that the software recognizes the date but returns the number of days since January 1, 1900.

Don't be concerned if your cell is formatted for numbers and you enter text and a number appears; simply format the cell and it will appear in the correct format. The software's standard format will be day/month/year. To modify this, go to the dialogue box below the number and change it to the desired order.

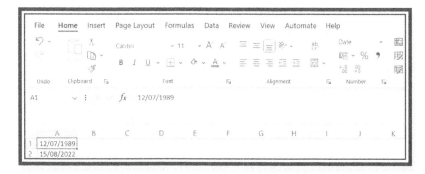

- **Line break**: Excel enables you to do so if you are entering text and do not want it to be a continuous line, but rather a broken one. On top of the worksheet, you will see a line that reads fx, which indicates where the cell's text (or formulas) are placed. Use the Alt+Enter key combination to determine where you want to break the text across multiple lines. This will move the cursor to the next line automatically. You may proceed as you see fit.

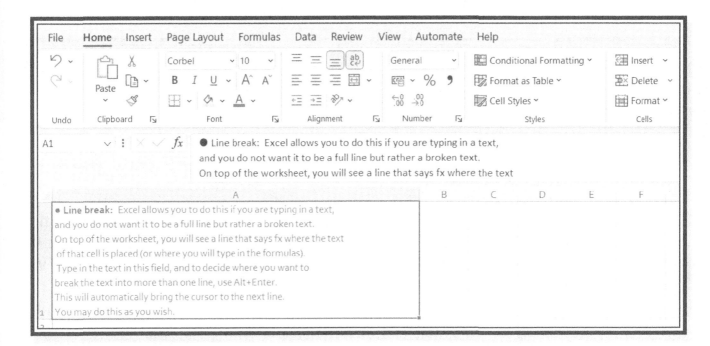

Pro tip: You can also use the **Wrap text** function in the **Alignment** section of the home tab to have the cell automatically adjust to its content. This will automatically **adjust the content** to the current column width of the spreadsheet and increase the line spacing. If you use the tip in the line break section, the cells will format themselves automatically.

FORMULAS AND FUNCTIONS

Formulas are one of the most important aspects of Excel and the primary reason it is used. As you already know, they are written using the bar at the top of the spreadsheet. You can use formulas in three distinct ways: by **manually entering** the formulas, as we will see in a moment; by going to the **function library** in the functions tab and selecting the type of formula you want to use; or by clicking the **fx** button, which will open a dialogue box with an assistant to help you fill in the formulas.

If you **enter the formula manually**, you must be aware that it must always begin with a mathematical symbol. The most common method is to begin with the **equal sign (=),** but you can also use the **plus (+)** or **minus (-)** signs. The asterisk **(*)**, which will be used for multiplication, and the forward slash (/), which will be used for division, cannot be used to initiate manual functions.

Pro tip: Consider that you are writing a text that begins with a '+', '-', or '=.' As you have seen, the software will automatically recognize this as a formula if you enter it. To prevent this and make the symbols visible, **you must add an apostrophe (') to the start of the text.** This will not appear on the text or printed document, but will indicate to the program that the formula should not be considered.

Hint: Although Excel provides a variety of formulas, you may wish to create the formula manually without referencing other cells. There is no difficulty involved. You can create a formula using the mathematical symbols on your keyboard as long as the formula begins with an equal sign (=). For instance, you may need to manually add 5, 7, and 9 by hand. There is no need to place each item in a separate cell. You only need to type =5+7+9.

AutoSum

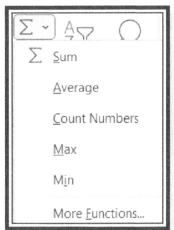

AutoSum will be the first set of formulas and functions examined. This button can be found in the **editing** section of the **home tab** as well as the first button on the formulas tab. The user will have access to the five most common Excel functions: **sum, average, count number, minimum, and maximum.** Let us examine each of them in detail.

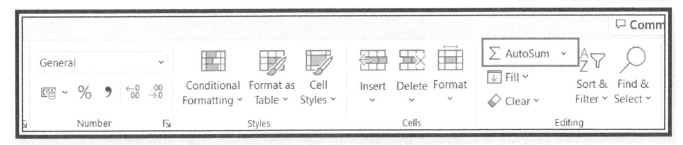

Consider the following list of jumbled numbers: 6, 15, 1, 27, 9, 3, 65, 87, 41, 2, and 7. They are located in column B, on lines 1 through 11. Therefore, line B1 contains the number 6, line B2 contains the number 15, etc. Although it may not seem crucial at first, the significance of each number's location will become clear in the following sections.

- **Sum**: The first thing we'll do is add these numbers together. Select the cell where you want the result to appear and click on the AutoSum icon's **Sum element**. If the cell you chose is directly beneath the numbers or on cell B12, it will automatically select the interval directly above it, or B1-B11. If the system does not select it automatically, you can do it manually.

  Keep in mind that the following formula will appear on the top bar: **=sum(B1:B11).** This will result in the following: Excel will compute the sum of the values in cells B1 through B11. When you've finished selecting the cells you want to add, press enter, and the result will appear automatically: 263.

- **Average:** The average function will have the same selection requirements as the sum function. However, in this case, the formula that will appear is: **=average(B1:B11**).

  This will result in the following once more: Excel will compute the average of the numbers in cells B1 through B11. You will click Enter once more (as you will for all formulas) and the result will appear: 23.90909.

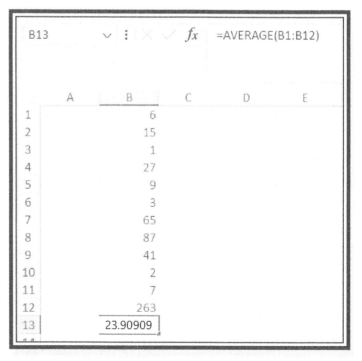

Pro tip: *As you might expect, the number in our average result is an ongoing decimal that will always be between 9 and 0. You can control how many decimal points appear in each cell. To do so, select the relevant cell and navigate to the* **number section in the home tab.** *The last two buttons have two zeroes written on them, each with an arrow pointing to the left and right. These are the* **buttons for reducing** *(arrow pointing left)* **or increasing** *(arrow pointing right) the number of decimal points displayed.*

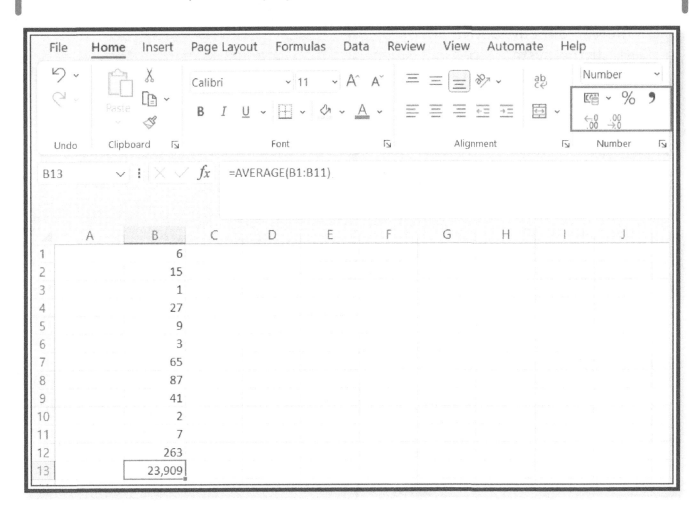

- **Count number:** This function will count the number of numbers in your selection. It is convenient to see the number of occurrences without having to manually count or perform calculations. **=count(B1:B11**) will be the formula. In this case, the answer is 11.

COUNT ⌄ ⋮ ✕ ✓ *fx* =COUNT(B1:B11)

	A	B	C	D	E
1		6			
2		15			
3		1			
4		27			
5		9			
6		3			
7		65			
8		87			
9		41			
10		2			
11		7			
12		=COUNT(B1:B11)			
13		COUNT(**value1**; [value2]; ...)			
14					
15					

- **Maximum:** Using the formula **=max(B1:B11),** this determines the number with the highest value within the specified range. The answer in our case is 87.

- **Minimum:** This, like the previous example, determines the minimum value within the range. The formula is as follows: **=min(B1:B11)**. The answer to the proposed example is 1.

B12 ⌄ ⋮ ✕ ✓ *fx* =MAX(B1:B11)

	A	B	C	D	E
1		6			
2		15			
3		1			
4		27			
5		9			
6		3			
7		65			
8		87			
9		41			
10		2			
11		7			
12		=MAX(B1:B11)			
13		MAX(**number1**; [number2]; ...)			

B12 ⌄ ⋮ ✕ ✓ *fx* =MIN(B1:B11)

	A	B	C	D	E
1		6			
2		15			
3		1			
4		27			
5		9			
6		3			
7		65			
8		87			
9		41			
10		2			
11		7			
12		=MIN(B1:B11)			
13		MIN(**number1**; [number2]; ...)			
14					

Pro tip: *Although we only used one column and one set of numbers in the previous examples, this can be done with multiple sets. As you may have noticed, the interval of B1:B11 is shared by all of the formulas.*

Now suppose you want to do the same thing with a range of numbers from lines 7 to 13 in column D. Both number selections must be entered into the formula. You can do this by holding down the Ctrl or Command key and selecting the other range. This will be reflected in the formula as a comma (,) separating both ranges. In this case, you will enter the formula's name and the range that you want it to calculate. The maximum function will be written as =max(B1:B11,D7:13).

Important! When typing formulas, no spaces should be used.

Financial Formulas

Excel is widely used in business to manage finances. The same thing happens to some people who prefer to manage their own money and investments. The software provides several formulas that can be used to accomplish this, and we will look at the five most important ones. All you have to do to see more **financial formulas** options is go to the **formulas tab** and click on the financial button.

Formulas Tab

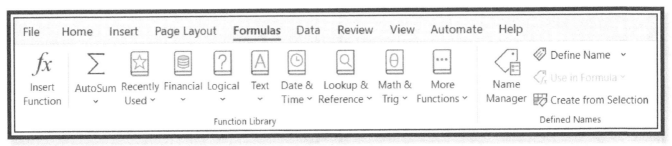

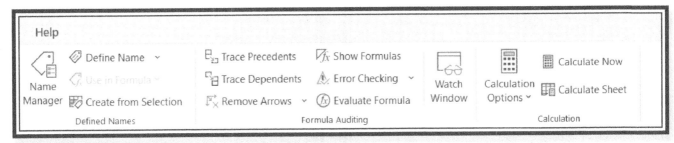

- **Yield:** This formula calculates the return on an investment over a specified time period. It can be used for either periodic or one-time payments.

The first item you'll need to include is the settlement, which is the date of the investment's settlement. This number, however, must be stated as a **serial date.** Remember how we said that dates that aren't configured to appear as dates bring in a whole number? That is the number you will require. Assume the settlement date is January 5, 2022; in this case, the serial number is 44,566.

You will now enter the **maturity date.** This must be expressed as a serial date number as well. Assume the date is 08/01/2024 in our scenario. This date's matching serial number is 45,299. The yearly rate of the coupon, which we can suppose is 6% or 0.06, should then be added. The software will next prompt you to enter the pr, which is the price of the security per $100 face value. In this scenario, we can multiply by $105. Finally, add the redemption, which will be the redemption value divided by the investment's face value of $100. Let's utilize $140 in this example.

Now that we have the basic information, we must determine the **frequency of the payments**. Excel will present you with shortcuts based on the frequency that you specify. We'll use two in this case to indicate a semiannual return. Finally, we will choose the number of days, or the basis, that will be used as the day count basis. In this situation, the number three will be used.

The result of your yield calculation will be 20%.

Function Arguments ? ✕

YIELD

Settlement	L14	⬆	=	44566
Maturity	L15	⬆	=	45299
Rate	L16	⬆	=	0,06
Pr	L17	⬆	=	105
Redemption	L18	⬆	=	140

=

Returns the yield on a security that pays periodic interest.

Redemption is the security's redemption value per $100 face value.

Formula result =

Help on this function   OK   Cancel

The final formula will look like this:

=YIELD(44566,45299,0.06,105,140,2,3)

Remember that while you can add these numbers manually, you can also create a table, that would look something like this:

		K	L
		K	**L**
14	Settlement date:	05/01/2022	
15	Maturity date:	08/01/2024	
16	Rate of interest:	6%	
17	Price per $100 FV:	105	
18	Redemption value:	140	
19	Payment terms	Semi-annual	

22°C
Sunny   🔍 Search   09:00 AM
01/09/202

| File | Home | Insert | Page Layout | Formulas | Data | Review | View | Automate | Help |

fx Insert Function

Σ AutoSum ˅
Recently Used ˅
Financial ˅

? Logical ˅
A Text ˅
Date & Time ˅

Lookup & Reference ˅
Math & Trig ˅
More Functions ˅

Define Name ˅
Use in Formula
Create from Selection

Trace Precedents
Trace Dependents
Remove Arrows

Name Manager

Function Library

Defined Names

YIELD ˅ ⋮ ✕ ✓ fx =YIELD(L14;L15;L16;L17;L18;2;3)

	F	G	H	I	J	K	L	M	N	O
13										
14						Settlement date:	05/01/2022			
15						Maturity date:	08/01/2024			
16						Rate of interest:	6%			
17						Price per $100 FV:	105			
18						Redemption value:	140			
19						Payment terms:	Semi-annual			
20							=YIELD(L14;L15;L16;L17;L18;2;3)			

The formula would look like this:

=YIELD(L14,L15,L16,L17,L18,2,3)

Pro tip: When applying this formula, you may receive the **'#NUM!' or '#VALUE!' error.** This indicates that something was not properly inserted in the formula. The '#VALUE!' issue could be caused by one of the parameters not being a number or by the settlement or maturity dates being invalid. If you receive the '#NUM!' error, it could be because the settlement date is greater than or equal to the maturity date, or because erroneous numbers were entered for an argument.

- **Price:** Let's imagine you have the yield but don't have the price of a securities. Excel can also assist you in determining this. We'll use the same numbers as in the last example. Only now, instead of utilizing the face value, which is what we want, we will include the yield in the table. The formula should be as follows:

=PRICE(44566,45299,0.06,0.2,140,2,3)

This calculation yields $105, which is the same as the number we had for face value in the first case. As a result, we may safely trust that our calculation is correct.

We can put the information in a table once more. It will seem as follows:

		K	L
14	Settlement date:	05/01/2022
15	Maturity date:	08/01/2024
16	Rate of interest:	6%
17	Yield	20%
18	Redemption value:	140
19	Payment terms	Semi-annual

And the formula will be this:

$$=PRICE(L14,L15,L16,L17,L18,2,3)$$

- **Rate:** Assume you want to apply for a loan but are unsure of the interest rate. Perhaps you'd like to know how much interest you'll have to pay over a set length of time for the amount you're asking for. In this scenario, the **rate formula** will be used. The first item you must include is the **Nper.** This is the number of loan or investment payment periods. Assume you will pay it off in two years, or 24 months. Then, write the Pmt, which is the payment that must be made throughout each month or the standard pay without interest. This figure will not change during the loan's term. Let's say the fixed figure in this scenario is $351. Because this is a loan, it is critical that a negative (-) sign appear in front of the number.

If you are requesting a loan, the pv field will need you to enter the loan amount into the formula. The amount in this scenario will be $6,000. The loan's future value is the next piece of information that must be included. It would not be used in this situation for a loan—it would be more appropriate to determine the interest rates of an investment, for example. As a result, we shall omit the value and enter zero. The same is true for the type—you will only be able to place it if you apply the investment formula. If this were the case, you'd have one for payment at the start of the term and zero for payment at the end. We shall use zero for our exercise.

22°C
Sunny
Search   W X P A O S N P
09:00 A
01/09/202

Finally, Excel will allow you to guess the rate. This will be represented with a decimal point denoting a percentage. You can omit the rate by guessing 0.1 (10%).

The final formula will look like this, and the answer is that the rate is 3%:

=RATE(24,-351,6000,0,0,0.1)

Once again, this information can be placed in a table.

	K	L
10	Payment:	Monthly
11	Loan amount:	6,000
12	Monthly payment:	351
13	Number of months:	24
14	Payments per year:	12

In this case, the formula would stay like this:

=RATE(L13,-L12,L11,0,0,0.1)

- **Nominal**: The nominal function is a basic financial calculation that determines the annual nominal interest rate of an application or loan. This formula is relatively basic and requires only two inputs. The first is the Effect rate, which is the application's effective interest rate. For this example, let's choose 16%, or 0.16. Following that, we must enter the Npery number, which represents the number of compounding periods per year. If the number we wish to know is relevant to one year, we enter the number 12. The ultimate figure will be 15%.

- **Variable Declining Balance (VDB)**: The VDB formula is especially useful for calculating the depreciation of an asset over time. Assume you want to buy a car but first want to know how much it will depreciate each day. The VDB formula should be used to determine how much value it will lose.

The first thing you need to include in the formula is the **cost**, or in our case, the price of the vehicle. Assume the car is worth $10,000. Following that, you will determine how much it would sell for after a year, possibly by searching for prices on the internet or asking the dealer. In our case, the car will be worth $13,000 at the end of a year—or the salvage will be worth this amount. The asset's life value will be determined by the estimated time of use. We can say ten years in this case.

The **start period** will be zero because it is the day you purchase the car, and the end period will be zero because we want to know the asset's daily depreciation. The factor is the rate of decline of the asset. You can leave it out entirely. The final result will be $8.22, and the formula will be as follows:

$$=VDB(15000,13000,10*365,0,1)$$

As a result, your answer will be that the car will depreciate at the rate of $8.22 per day from the day you buy it. Consider the following when looking at it in a table:

	K	L
10	Initial cost:	15.000
11	Salvage:	13.000
12	Life:	10 years

$$=VDB(L10,L11,L12*365,0,1)$$

Logical Formulas

Logical formulas are especially useful when attempting to combine two or more formulas. Excel gives the user a plethora of options for making calculations easier, so they don't have to keep adding multiple formulas to different cells. Let's look at a few of them.

- **AND**: The **AND formula** will be used to join two or more logical references. This formula will allow you to determine whether a particular argument is **TRUE** and, if so, whether the response is TRUE.

  If you type 1>2, for example, the result will be FALSE because the assumption is incorrect. However, if you put that 2>1, the answer is correct. If you use the formula **=AND(1>2,2>1)** to combine these two assumptions, the answer will be FALSE because one of them is incorrect.

  However, if the formula is written as **=AND(3>2,2>1)**, the result is TRUE because all of the assumptions are correct. This formula allows the user to validate a series of logical issues within their spreadsheet and return the correct answer. As is customary, inputs can be made manually or by selecting specific cells.

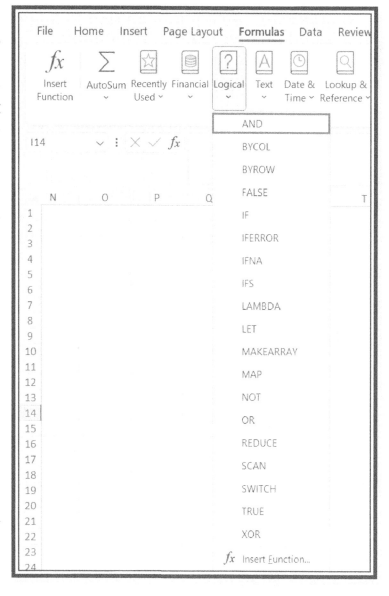

- **OR**: The arguments for the **OR formula** are similar to those for the AND formula. In this case, however, you will be using that different formulas can occur in distinct instances: this OR that. The OR function will also return TRUE or FALSE depending on the arguments. If one of the statements is true and the other is false, the outcome is TRUE. On the other hand, the answer will be FALSE only if all of the results are FALSE.

- **IFERROR:** You can use this formula to determine whether or not the value of the expression contains an error. It is typically used to validate answers when your formula results are **'#NUM!', '#VALUE!', '#REF!', '#NAME?',** or other similar characters. This is a logical function that can be incorporated into a formula or cell. Assume we add the formula =12/0 to a cell. Excel will give us the answer #DIV/0!. We use IFERROR to figure out what went wrong with the formula. If there is an error in the formula, we want it to tell us that it is 'incorrect.'

  The formula will be as follows: **=IFERROR(L15,"incorrect")**. In this case, L15 is the cell containing the error, and 'incorrect' is what we want the program to return if the result is incorrect. The cell response should be false.

  Pro tip: *When entering letters into a formula, make sure to put them between quotation marks (" and ") so that the result is text.*

- **COUNTIF:** The **COUNTIF function** can be highly advantageous when attempting to determine the quantity of elements contained within a specified range. For instance, consider a set of arbitrary numerical values, wherein certain numbers occur more than once, as illustrated in the subsequent sequence:

  The sequence of numbers provided by the user is as follows: 6, 15, 1, 27, 9, 1, 3, 65, 87, 1, 41, 2, and 7. It is evident that the number one appears multiple times in the sequence, and it is necessary to determine the frequency of its repetition. Let us consider the hypothetical scenario where the entities in question are situated within the range of cells B4 to B17. In order to utilize the countif formula, the syntax will be as follows:

  =COUNTIF(B4:B17,1)

  The range of cells from B4 to B17 contains the numerical values, while the number 1 is the target value being sought. In this particular instance, the correct response would be three, as the numeral one is observed to occur thrice within the given sequence. This formula is particularly advantageous when dealing with a substantial volume of data that is not amenable to reorganization, and the objective is to determine the frequency of information occurrences. This tool has the capability to be utilized with both textual data and numerical values.

- **IF**: The **IF formula** is widely recognized and frequently utilized in Microsoft Excel. The tool has multiple applications, one of which involves verifying the data that has been inputted into the spreadsheet. Let us consider a straightforward example that has been previously encountered. Assuming a lack of knowledge regarding the solution to the inequality 1>2. In this particular scenario, we will incorporate this logical reasoning into the formula. In the logical_test, the expression "1>2" will be written. The subsequent procedure involves specifying the expected output of the program in the event that the given condition is satisfied. For illustrative purposes, the term 'CORRECT' will be employed. The final step involves specifying the desired return value in the event that the answer is determined to be FALSE. In this case, the term 'RECALCULATE' will be designated for this purpose. The formula will be represented as follows:

=IF(1>2,"CORRECT","RECALCULATE")

As a result of Excel's conclusion that 1>2 is incorrect, this will be the solution. If we were to reverse the answer—2>1—the following formula would be used:

=IF(2>1,"CORRECT","RECALCULATE")

The computer would then display the word "CORRECT" in the cell. This formula can be used in other cells, where the other values will be determined by your preference and the cell number will serve as the location of the logical test.

Pro tip: *Did you know that if you select and drag a formula that is already present in a cell, it will be duplicated? Additionally, this implies that the references will be repeated. However, there are times when we prefer one cell to remain the same throughout all calculations while the others change. This can be accomplished by using the $ symbol to "lock" the cell number you want to stay the same. Say, for instance, that you want to copy the same formula from cell B1 to cells B2 to B5. You would naturally want to drag the information, am I right? What if the formula on B1 reads =ADD(A1:A7)?*

The formula would also change if you moved the cell. It would be of the form =ADD(A2:A8) on B2, =ADD(A3:A9) on B3, and so forth. In this instance, you would put the cells in B1: =ADD($A$1:$A$7) to 'lock' them. This indicates that both the column and the line number are locked. You would only use the $ symbol in front of the letters if you only wanted to keep the columns, and you would only use it in front of the numbers if you only wanted to keep the line numbers.

Text Formulas

- **CLEAN**: Clean is a function that gets right to the point. It will eliminate all of the text's non-printable characters from your spreadsheet.

  Consider removing all the spaces from a text that you pasted into Excel. Simply enter (or press return) after typing a space in the text field.

  The worksheet's spaces will then all be automatically deleted by the program. The equation would be as follows:

  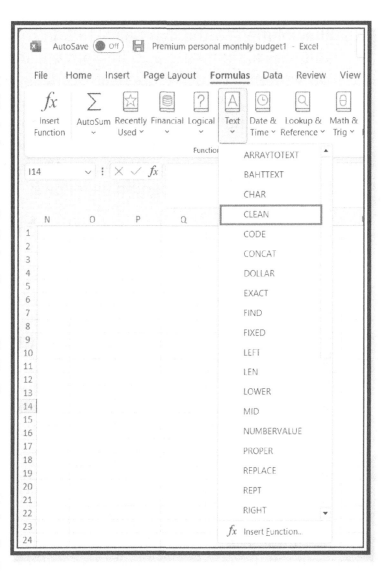

$$=CLEAN(" ")$$

- **CONCATENATE**: Consider that you are entering a number range in a spreadsheet with each number being entered in a different cell. You do, however, want them to be kept together in a single cell for whatever reason. Not to worry! You won't need to type them out one at a time.

  The **CONCATENATE formula** can be used. You can choose these in the order you want to arrange them if, for instance, your data is in cells C4 to C16. Perhaps all you want to do is group cells C4, C7, and C11 together. In this situation, your formula will appear as follows:

$$=CONCATENATE(C4,C7,C11)$$

The same holds true when using words or constructing sentences. Consider that the words CAR, DRIVE, and ROAD are present. The formula is as follows if you choose the cells where they are located:

$$=CONCATENATE("CAR","DRIVE","ROAD")$$

The outcome will be as follows: CARDRIVEROAD. Have you observed that, in this particular instance, there is an absence of a space? In order to include punctuation or spaces, it is necessary to incorporate them within the formula. Let us examine the formula with the aforementioned modifications, all of which have been implemented within the confines of the quotation marks.

$$=CONCATENATE("CAR ","DRIVE. ","ROAD!")$$

The outcome, in this particular instance, will be the operation of a motor vehicle. The term "road" is used to refer to a paved or unpaved pathway designed for As evident, one has the capacity to employ their imaginative faculties to interconnect any desired information, whether it pertains to cellular structures or arbitrary lexical units.

- **REPLACE:** The replace formula is precisely as its name implies. The user will initiate a request for Excel to replace a specific value with another value by utilizing a formula. Initially, the user is required to designate a specific textual element, such as the term **"FALSE,"** that necessitates the substitution of certain constituent characters.

Subsequently, the user will designate the position within the word, denoted by a numerical value, at which the desired character is to be substituted, referred to as the start_num. In this particular scenario, our objective is to replace the letter 'E'. In this particular instance, the numerical value that is required for placement is 5. Subsequently, the num_chars parameter will be ascertained, representing the quantity of characters within the original text that are intended to be substituted, specifically one character in the given illustration. Finally, the subsequent step involves the insertion of the desired additional text, specifically, the third piece of text in our particular scenario. The formula should be as follows:

=REPLACE(FALSE,5,1,3)

The outcome of our analysis will be denoted as 'FALSE.' This feature is highly advantageous for the replacement of numerous characters within an extensive text or a dataset that is already present within a spreadsheet.

- **SEARCH:** The **search algorithm** will provide the user with the desired value within a specified cell or a designated range of cells. The formula employed in this context is insensitive to case, thereby disregarding any differentiation between uppercase and lowercase characters.

  The initial requirement in the equation necessitates the inclusion of the find_text, which denotes the specific text that is sought after. In the present illustration, the letter A will be employed. The text in question, from which we aim to identify the element, is "THE CAR IS DRIVING DOWN THE ROAD."

  The aforementioned element will be positioned in the field designated as within_text. In the final stage, it is desired that the software provides the positional index of the letter 'A' from the initial position. Consequently, the user will input '1' or leave the field blank, as the absence of an alternative will default the starting position to 1. The formula can be represented as follows:

  =SEARCH("A","THECARISDRIVINGDOWNTHEROAD",1)

  And the result will be 5 because the first letter A is in position 5 in reference to the sentence.

- **FIND:** In contrast to the search formula, the **find function** exhibits case sensitivity, thereby distinguishing between uppercase and lowercase characters. The initial requirement in the equation necessitates the inclusion of the find_text, denoting the specific text that is sought after. Let us consider the utilization of the letter A once more. The text in which we aim to identify the element is "The car is driving down the road." The aforementioned element will be positioned in the field designated as within_text.

  The formula can be represented as follows:

=FIND("A","THECARISDRIVINGDOWNTHEROAD",1)

The outcome will be 5 as the initial letter "A" is situated in the fifth position relative to the sentence. However, in the event that we were conducting a search for the lowercase letter 'a,' the outcome would yield an error denoted as '#VALUE!'. This is due to the absence of the lowercase letter 'a' within the sentence under examination.

Date and Time Formulas

The utilization of date and time formulas may appear straightforward when performed manually, yet their practicality becomes evident when working with data organized in rows and columns that are categorized by years, months, and days.

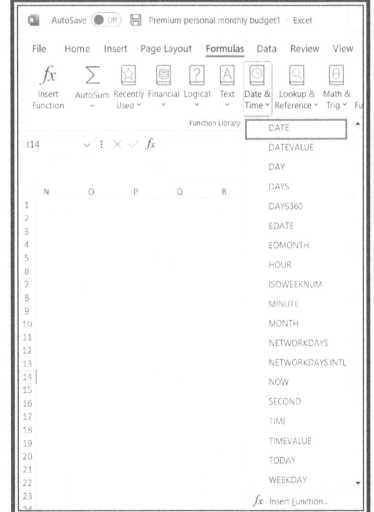

Additionally, there are several advantageous functionalities that facilitate the automatic daily updating of your document, eliminating the need for manual intervention. The following items are included.

- **DATE:** This formula will be particularly helpful in the situations mentioned above where you have multiple rows of data with year, month, and day separations. Actually, the formula is quite straightforward:

=DATE(YEAR,MONTH,DAY)

In this instance, fill in the year in the first cell, the month in the second, and the day in the third. Your solution will be returned if you drag it down without locking the cells, and it will include all three columns in date format. Assume that the day is on B5, the month is on C5, and the year is on B5. Your formula will then appear as follows:

=DATE(B5,C5,D5)

- **TODAY:** You don't need to add anything to the parenthesis in the formula of today. Instead, you can add a formula to your table that will update each time you open the worksheet. The calculation is easy:

=TODAY()

When you do this, the worksheet will display the current date and update to the next day's date when you open it. If you have a document that you update every day and print, this formula is especially helpful. Using this formula, you can have a dated document printed every day without having to manually change the date each time you open it.

TIME: The time formula above and the time formula are very similar. The hour, minute, and second should be added here in place of the day, month, and year. The formula is straightforward once more:

=TIME(HOUR,MINUTE,SECOND)

- The steps you entered into the date formula are the same ones that will be used, so if you have one, you also have the other.

Pro tip: Keep in mind to format the cells in this manner before using the date or time formulas. There are a number to pick from, and your decision will be based on your preferences and intended uses. Just select all the cells you want to change at once, then click the drop-down menu next to the number section on the home tab to format them all at once.

- **NETWORKDAYS**: This is the formula to use if you want to know how many workdays you will have in a given period of time.

22°C Sunny   🔍 Search   W X P A O S T N P   09:00 AM 01/09/202

You can specify the **start_date** you want to start with and the **end_date** of the period by using the networkdays function. For the software to recognize them, these must be expressed as serial numbers. Following the placement of both entries, you can add the serial number that refers to the holidays on which you will not be working in the field below. You will see the total number of labor days for that time period after pressing enter. The equation will appear as follows:

$$\text{=NETWORKDAYS(START\_DATE,END\_DATE,(HOLIDAYS))}$$

- **YEAR**: If you need to convert a group of years that have been formatted as serial numbers, this formula will be especially helpful. You only need to enter the serial number in reference for the formula to return the year to you. It goes like this:

$$\text{=YEAR(SERIAL\_NUMBER)}$$

Reference Formulas

If you are employed in a corporate setting, you have probably already heard someone mention using a **"VLOOKUP"** formula.

Although some people may think this is difficult, rest assured that it is not. One of Excel's many reference formulas, this one enables you to search for data across one or more sheets.

Continue reading to learn more and you will be able to get all of your questions about this well-known formula and others answered.

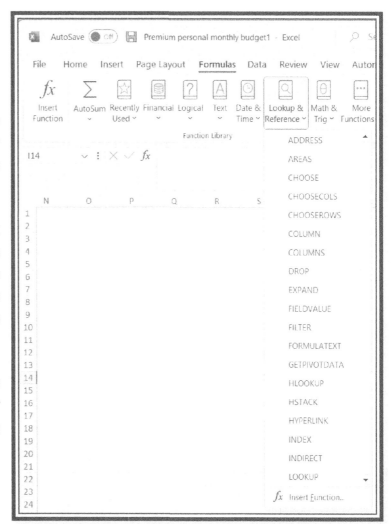

- **HLOOKUP**: We can say that the **hlookup function** is the less well-known sibling of the vlookup function. The user of this formula can search for a value in a data table and have it returned in the line that you specify. Let's say the name of a month from the year is on line 1 in each of the columns from A to L. As a result, the fields A1:L1 will be filled in, and we will be searching only within these fields.

  The **lookup_value**, which in this case will be "March," must be put in first. The next step is to instruct Excel where to look for the data or table you require. Let's assume that the information needed for this exercise is present in all the lines up to 10. This indicates that the **table_array**, or the table in which we will be looking for the information, will be A1:L1o.

  Finally, using the **row_index_num**, we will inform the system of which line we want the reference to appear. Line 3 contains numbers from 1 to 12, which we will use in this situation to indicate that we want the information provided to us. Not to mention, we will decide whether we want an exact match to be discovered (FALSE) or a rough result based on ascending order (TRUE). The formula should appear as follows:

  =HLOOKUP("March",A1:L10,3,FALSE)

  The result that should come back to you is number 3.

- **VLOOKUP**: Now let's examine the well-known **vlookup.** This formula enables the user to look for a value, just like the hlookup does. The difference is that it will take into account the information in a table of values and return it in the column that you specify. To make things clear, let's use the same illustration as before.

  Consider that each month's name from rows 1 to 12 is in column A. This indicates that the fields we will be searching within, **A1–A12**, will be filled in.

  The lookup_value, which in this case will be "March," must be entered first. The next step is to instruct Excel where to look for the data or table you require. Let's assume for the sake of this exercise that information is present in every column up until the letter L. This indicates that the table or table_array in which we will look for the data will be A1:L12.

22°C
Sunny

Search   W   X   P   A   O   S   T   N   P

09:00 A
01/09/202

The system will then be informed of the line in which we want the reference to appear, in this case the column_index_num. In this case, we want to receive the data from column E (or column 5), which contains numbers from 1 to 12. Not to mention, we will decide whether we want an exact match to be discovered **(FALSE)** or a rough result based on ascending order **(TRUE)**. The formula should appear as follows:

=HLOOKUP("March",A1:L12,5,FALSE)

The result that should come back to you is number 3.

Pro tip: If the vlookup and hlookup functions seem difficult to comprehend, perhaps this additional explanation will help. In both situations, we are interested in knowing the results that a specific row or number will give us when we search for a particular value. In the examples we used, we looked for the month of March, but in reality, we were more interested in learning what number this month stood for overall.

If you need to search through a large data table for a specific piece of information, these formulas will be especially helpful. Another illustration would be if we had a table with the grades students received for a test that covered seven different subjects. We're interested in the outcomes of a student by the name of Claire. For instance, depending on the information's format, we could use a vlookup or hlookup formula to bring all of Claire's grades into evidence without filtering. Only the row or line number will change in this scenario; the formula will remain unchanged.

- **MATCH**: The position of an item within a dataset that **matches a particular value** you are looking for within a specific order is returned by the match function. Identifying the lookup_value is the first step you must take. The **table_array** will then be put in place. Last but not least, you'll need to enter a value—1, 0, or -1—to indicate what you want to return.

  The largest value that is less than or equal to the value you're looking for will be found using a number 1 or a match. If you add a 0, the match will find the value that is exactly the same as the one you are looking for—the order of the table is irrelevant.

If you add a -1, the match will find the smallest value that is greater than or equal to the value you are searching for—as long as the information table is arranged in descending order.

- **TRANSPOSE**: You can organize your data by using the **transpose formula**. Let's say you want to change the information from being all in one column to being in a line format. Simply choose the range in which the information is located, click on the line where the change is to be made, and then press enter to complete the change. The same applies if you want to change a line into a column in the opposite circumstance. This formula can also be used in this situation to turn the horizontal data vertical.

- **FORMULATEXT**: One of the most helpful formulas and crucial ones to remember was saved for last. This is how the **formulatext** works. This function's task is to identify the formula used in a given cell. Have you ever received a spreadsheet where the formula was unclear or the information's source was unclear? You won't have this issue any longer, then. If you click on an empty cell and then use the formulatext, you can choose the cell that contains the calculation you're having trouble figuring out and then press enter to receive the answer right away—it's like magic!

DATA VALIDATION, TRANSFORMING TEXT, AND FILTERING

The chapter's next section will cover the use of filters, data validation, and text transformation—all helpful features when sharing Excel with multiple users. You can use these to organize and find the data you have in your spreadsheet by filtering it.

Data Tab

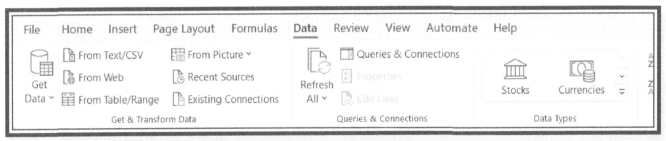

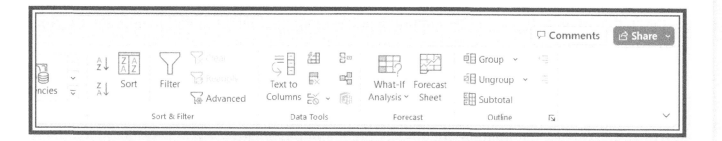

DATA VALIDATION

You can restrict the user's options when filling out a specific cell using the **data validation tool.** You can choose whether the item to be placed is going to be a whole number, a decimal, a list, a date, a time, a text message of a certain length, or a personalized message. Assume you want to make a list with a predetermined range of numbers that a third party can only select from. In this scenario, you would choose the list from the drop-down menu and then choose the list's source.

You must have the list in a location where Excel can read from it, either in the same spreadsheet or a different one, for this feature to function. When the mouse is over the source, you can select the data set to which you want to limit the user and then press enter. When the user clicks on that cell, the list is then generated and appears as a **drop-down menu.** The only permitted values will be those that are contained there.

If you choose to use any of the other options, you can also add your own messages, such as the one that should appear if the wrong text is entered or one that will be displayed when you click on a cell. The data validation button, which is found on the data tab of the ribbon, will be where all of these features are established.

TRANSFORMING TEXT

To make use of your Excel spreadsheet more effectively, there may be a time when you want to copy the data that is stored elsewhere. The majority of the time, though, this information will be misconfigured after being pasted. For instance, if you copy a table from a.pdf file into the program, it probably won't recognize the original document's columns that distinguished the information and will instead combine everything into a single line. You shouldn't worry, though. For this, Excel has a feature called **text to columns.**

This button can also be found on the ribbon's **data tab**, in the data tools section. Selecting the text you want to transform is the first step in using it. After choosing, select the drop-down menu by clicking the text-to-column button. You must choose just one column because this tool can only be used for one table at a time.

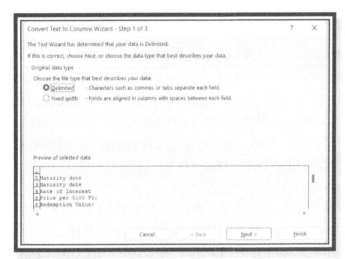

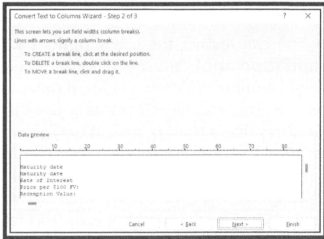

You must identify the information when the dialogue box opens. You must decide whether the fields are **delimited**, in which case commas and spaces are used to demarcate them, or if they have a **fixed width**, in which case the text is neatly aligned with spaces between each field.

Let's say your data is disorganized and the semicolons serve as dividers. You will be directed to a different screen on the dialogue box after choosing this option, where you must choose the common separator between each field. You have the option of adding your own options in addition to the ones the program provides.

22°C Sunny   Search   W X P A O S T N P   09:00 AM 01/09/202

Excel will ask where you want this data to be placed after you choose the separator and **click next** (remember to leave empty columns after this so there is room for the information), and then you can click finish. The information will once more be divided into columns and used in the same way as the original document.

Pro tip: The remaining spaces can be filled in using the find and replace tool or the clear formula.

HOW TO SORT AND SET FILTER

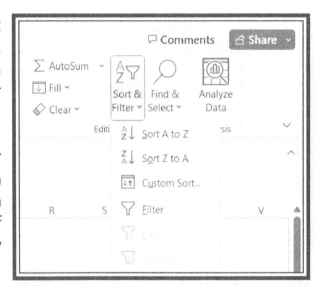

Excel filtering involves much more than just choosing the particular data you want to see. There are a variety of options available when filtering, including filter by cell color, number the filters, filter by cell format, and more.

Click the header of the information in your spreadsheet and select the Sort & Filter option from the Home tab of the ribbon to apply a filter. After selecting the filter option, each of the top data-containing cells will have a tiny arrow in a gray box appear on its corner.

From there, you can sort your data and apply filters based on values or empty values.

Pro tip: It is crucial to have headings when using a filter so that the tool can take into account all of the data. This will also be necessary for making a number of other tools, such as graphs and pivot tables, as you will see in the following section. In light of this, it is typically a good idea to have a heading before entering the data on the worksheet.

CREATE PIVOT TABLES

The final Excel tool you should be aware of is creating **Pivot Tables**. If you have never used or seen one, they are fairly simple. Large data sets can be organized using pivot tables, which also produce a dynamic visualization of your data that is more approachable. They will be useful, especially if your table contains thousands of data points that you cannot comprehend or relate. With the aid of this tool, you can sort the data and even make interactive graphs.

The pivot table button must first be selected by going to the **insert tab on the ribbon.** When a drop-down menu with options appears, **choose PivotTable from the table or range.** The dialog box will open, and the cursor will move to the table/range bar. You will then be able to choose the data table you want to work with. Next, you must choose whether the newly created pivot table belongs in the current worksheet or in a new worksheet (recommended if there is information on the other worksheets). After that, all you have to do is click "OK" to get a table with all the data you require.

Insert Tab

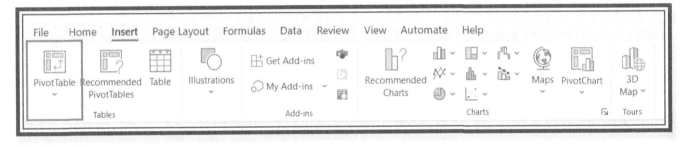

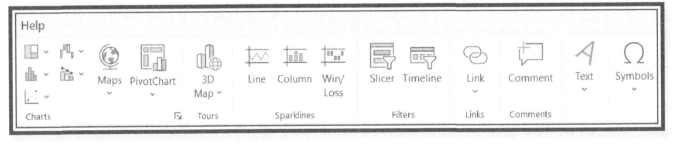

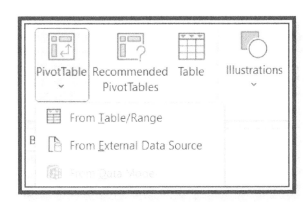

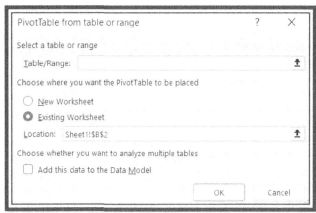

The workspace of the new worksheet will have room for the table, and a bar labeled **PivotTable Fields** will be visible to the left of the workspace.

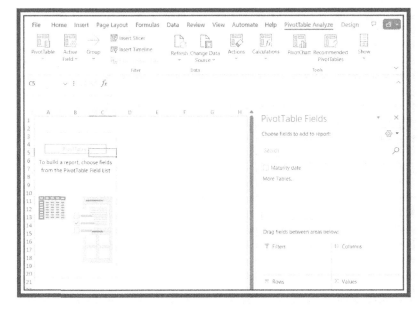

Here, the headings demonstrate their value because using them will make it simple for you to locate the information in the table that you are looking for. The list of all the fields you can select is located in the first and largest square. You only need to drag them to each of the four **fields—filters, columns, rows**, and values—on the bottom of the task panel to decide whether or not you want to use them. From there, you can play around with, test, and move the data that will be displayed in the workspace automatically.

> **Pro tip:** *Excel will give you the option to make additional calculations with the data displayed in the **values field.** The data can be combined, averaged, counted, or even used to find the product. The options for summarizing and displaying the field will be displayed in a dialogue box when you click the black arrow that appears on the line's extreme right and select **Value Field Settings.** The data can be formatted in the workspace to resemble a typical spreadsheet.*

KEYBOARD SHORTCUTS

FUNCTION	SHORTCUT ON PC	SHORTCUT ON MAC
Undo action	Ctrl + Z	Command + Z
Center align cell contents	Alt + H, A, C	Command + E
Edit cell	F2	F2
Lock formula	F4	F4
Add line or column	Ctrl + +	Command + +
Delete line or column	Ctrl + -	Command + -
Hide selected row	Ctrl + 9	Command + (
Hide selected column	Ctrl + 0	Command +)
Go to formula tab	Alt + M	Command + Shift + U
Move cells in worksheet	Arrow keys	Arrow keys
Move to beginning of sheet	Ctrl + home	Command + home
Zoom in	Ctrl + Alt + =	Not available
Zoom out	Ctrl + Alt + -	Not available
Extend selection	Ctrl + Shift + Down arrow	Shift + Command + down arrow
Fill selected range with current entry	Ctrl + Enter	Command + return
Repeat last command	Ctrl + Y	Command + Y
Display function arguments	Ctrl + A	Command + A
Refresh data	Ctrl + F5	Command + F5

22°C Sunny    Search   09:00 AM 01/09/2023

Section 3:
Microsoft POWERPOINT

You might spend a significant amount of time each day preparing presentations. Even though there are currently a number of tools available to do this, **Microsoft PowerPoint** is still the method of choice for many. This tool still offers the most resources for such presentations, whether they are for business or personal use. Let's look at some of the software's main features and how they can be applied. As was already mentioned, some of the formatting and inserting tools it offers are comparable to those in Excel and Word; therefore, if you have any questions, please refer to the book's first two chapters.

CREATING A PRESENTATION

Powerpoint will automatically open a blank slide when you open a new file, allowing you to add a title and a subtitle. This will be the start of a presentation that you will design for yourself using the required text, images, and other resources. The page's initial design is straightforward as you can see: The options slide is in the center of the screen, and a scroll bar to the left allows you to view every slide in your presentation.

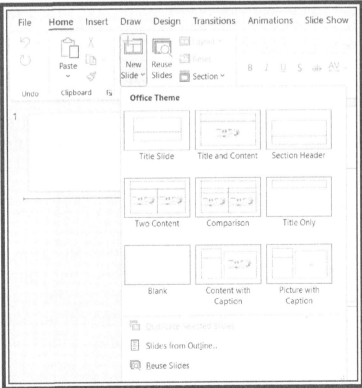

You have three choices if you want to add new slides:

1. Click on **new slide** on the **slides** section of the ribbon in the home tab.

2. Click on **new slide** on the **slides** button of the **insert** tab of the ribbon.

3. Click on the **slide thumbnail panel** (to the left) of the presentation with the right button and select **new slide**.

A predefined slide with space for adding titles and text will automatically appear when you add a new slide. To style them appropriately, use the text formatting tools on the **ribbon's home tab.**

Home Tab

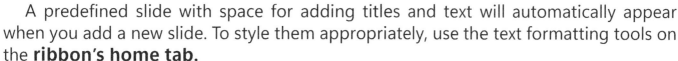

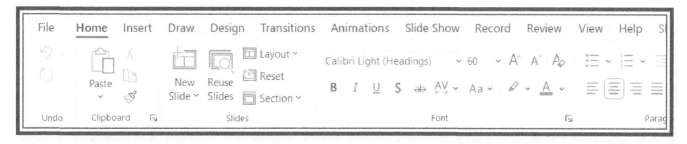

But let's say you want to alter the slide's design because you don't like it. There are two ways to alter this design in PowerPoint:

The first is by selecting the layout button in the home tab's slides section. The alternative is to use your mouse's right button to select a layout by clicking on the window containing the slide you wish to change.

The software will give you a variety of layouts if you apply a style, which is covered in more

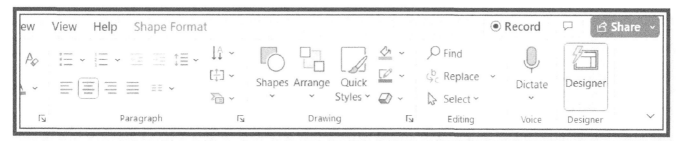

detail in the following chapter. Powerpoint will just give you different boxes to apply the format you want if there isn't a style applied.

Pro tip: *ABy selecting the location you want to insert the slide in the thumbnail panel, you can add new slides anywhere in your presentation, including the middle. All you have to do to start a new slide is click the right mouse button when a red line between the slides should appear.*

Shifting objects around

It's simpler than you might think to manage the slides in Excel because everything is done through the **thumbnail panel** on the left side of your screen. You must first be aware that this panel can be scrolled up and down so you can see which slides make up your presentation.

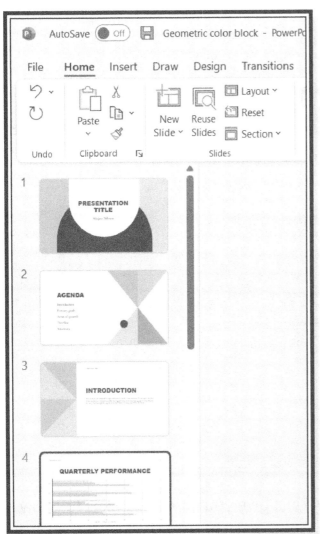

As a result, all you have to do to move a slide is click on the slide you want to move and **drag and drop** it between the other slides that will appear. You won't have to worry about deleting or starting over, which will make managing the presentation easier.

The procedure is essentially the same to **remove a slide.** The slide you want to delete should be selected in the thumbnail panel by clicking its right button. When a menu appears, choose delete slide from it. (See the image on top in the next page.)

Selecting the slide and pressing the **delete key on your keyboard** are additional options. If you accidentally did it, don't be concerned. You can undo something by pressing the undo key on your keyboard or using the undo feature on the ribbon.

22°C
Sunny

Search

09:00 AM
01/09/2023

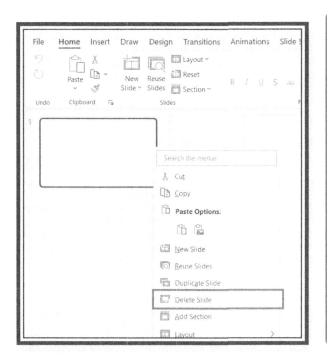

Pro tip: *When you open a PowerPoint template, you will notice that the slide has a dotted line. This line will not be included in your presentation. It is instead used to define the area to which you will add text, images, or whatever other content you choose.*

By clicking on the line and dragging it to the desired size, you can increase or decrease the size of this work area. To add a dialogue box to insert text, simply click the text box button in the text section of the insert tab of the ribbon.

Insert Tab

22°C
Sunny
🔍 Search

09:00 AM
01/09/2023
105

APPLYING THEMES

Companies will sometimes provide a template for all employees to use in their presentations. If this is not the case for you, don't worry: PowerPoint allows users to apply one of its available themes and templates in situations like these. Continue reading to learn about the differences between them and how to choose the best one for your presentation.

Themes

When you decide to begin a presentation, you can choose a theme for it. This means that PowerPoint will automatically select a set of fonts, colors, styles, and visual effects for your presentation. These options are available in the ribbon's **design tab**, under the themes section. There, you will find several standard presentation styles and their potential variations.

Design Tab

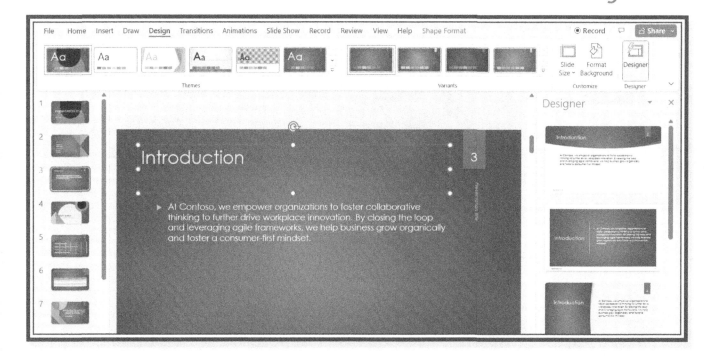

While the program already includes some options, you can search the internet for others by clicking on the down arrow to the right side of the theme box. As you add new slides, you'll notice that the formatting remains consistent. However, if you want to change the layout but are afraid of making changes, don't worry. If you use one of the above steps to add a new layout, the program will automatically present you with pre-formatted layout options from which to choose.

Essentially, using a theme is appropriate when you already know what you want to include in your presentation and do not require any guidance on what and how to include. It will allow you to add your ideas creatively and freely by establishing a standardized format. Using the theme tool, as opposed to the template function, will give you some direction while allowing you to establish the flow of the presentation..

Templates

File Tab

The **templates** in PowerPoint can be found in the document's **file tab.** The software displays several options to the user and allows you to select one online.

Keep in mind that these are not determined for each situation that the user may desire, but rather for how you want the presentation to look. Please keep in mind that while some of these themes have over 20 slide options, others have fewer.

It is also worth noting that some of these styles will provide you with a clear outline for your presentation. You don't have to follow them exactly, and you can change them to suit your needs.

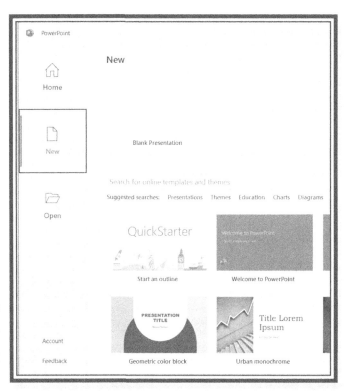

Building a Master Presentation

Assume your company has assigned you to create a standard template for the entire company to use, or that you want to create one for your business or school. By enabling the master slide feature in PowerPoint, you can achieve the same result. When you include a **new slide**, everything is already set up for you if you use a template or a style. This is the master slide feature in action.

You can design a template for your company that includes a logo, font, colors, chart styles, and image placeholders for other users. To access the master view, navigate to the view tab on the ribbon and then click the **slide master button** within the master view section. When you do this, the ribbon changes and all of the features that appear are solely related to the master slides.

View Tab

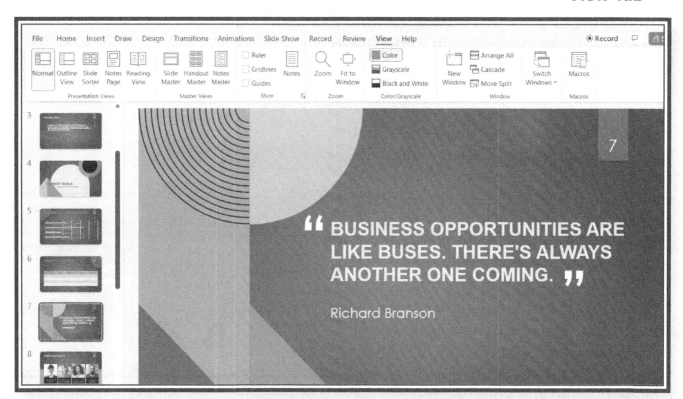

Here you can customize the appearance of the opening slide, create different designs for the remaining slides, add page numbers and dates, and even add specific themes

from the PowerPoint library. Remember that everything you do on the ribbon while the master view is open will be related to the master slides. To return to the presentation, go to the **slide master tab** and click the **close master view button.**

Slide Master Tab

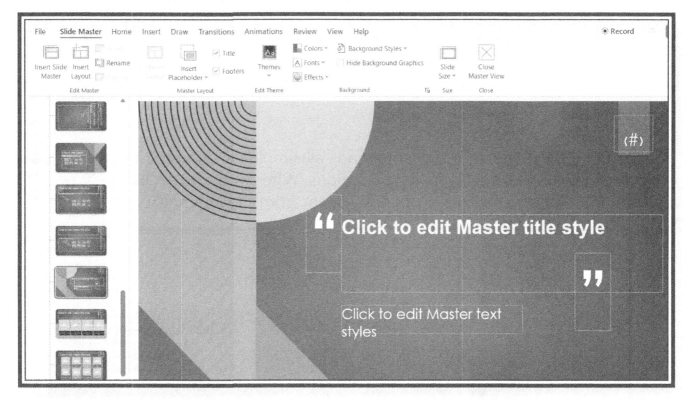

Pro tip: *Once you've styled the master view to your liking, every new addition you make to the presentation will be based on it, including the layouts, font, and overall appearance. You can either create a new master template from scratch or modify an existing one, depending on your preferences.*

MANAGE AND INSERTING PICTURES, CLIPARTS, AND VIDEOS

When creating a presentation, you may need to include a picture, an icon, or even a video to illustrate your point. This is not a problem for PowerPoint users because the software allows them to include a variety of objects within the presentation and make them interactive while presenting. If you open a new slide other than the first one in the newer versions of Powerpoint, you will see eight small icons available in the text box from which to choose. They are made up of a table, a graph, a form, a 3D object, images, online images, or an icon.

Inserting Pictures

Inserting a **picture** into a presentation is as simple as using the **copy and paste** options, keyboard shortcuts, or ribbon options. When you add an image, PowerPoint allows you to select a file from your computer or from the internet.

The same procedure is followed when adding shapes or SmartArt. Remember that these will be initially placed within the slide's work area. Increase the work area or click on the image to **drag and resize it**, using the shift button to maintain its proportions, to resize them and have them auto-adjust.

Another option provided by the software is the ability to attach a photo album to a specific slide. These are useful when you need to illustrate a slide with more than one image but don't want to show them all at once. In the images section of the **insert tab, you can insert one of these albums.**

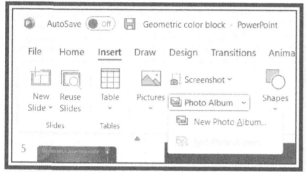

When you click the button, a dialogue box will appear, allowing you to select which images to include.

In this case, they must be saved on your computer so that the program can locate them. To look for these images, navigate to the **file/disk option.** You can include as many as you want depending on the size of your presentation. There will also be options for how to fit the images to the slide, whether or not to add captions, and the shape of the album.

When you add an album, it will appear in the selected slide. You must **click or press** enter to make the images appear and change during the presentation. These image features will allow you to make your presentation friendlier and less text-heavy, capturing the attention of those in attendance and adding a colorful element to the picture.

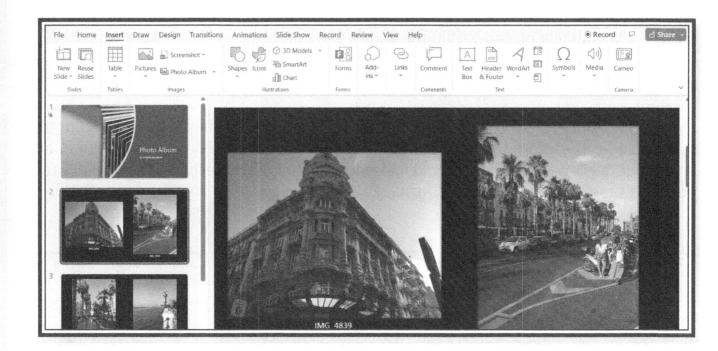

Inserting Videos and Sound

Inserting video and sound into your presentation may appear difficult, but it is actually quite simple. You can add videos from the internet without having to download them to your computer, or you can add a video from your hard drive. Sound files must be saved on your computer before they can be uploaded when you select them.

Let's start with videos, which are a fantastic way to add more life to your presentation. You cannot use the copy and paste feature in these cases. Instead, use the **insert video** feature in the media section of the insert tab. When you click the down-pointing arrow, you will be asked whether you want to upload a video from your device or use an online source.

The process will be similar to adding a picture if you use a media feature stored on your computer.

Insert Tab

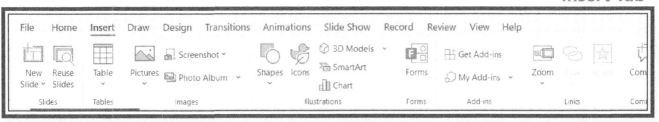

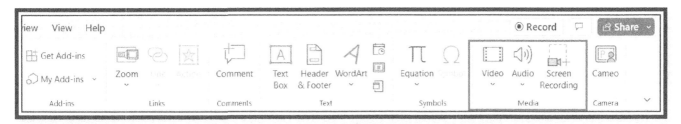

If you prefer to source the video directly from the internet, you can do so through a variety of platforms, including YouTube, Vimeo, SlideShare, Stream, and Flip. Because the software only supports these platforms, they are the only ones from which you can choose. You must use your default browser to find the video in one of the supported channels. Once you've found it, copy the address that appears in your browser's navigation bar and paste it into the field with a magnifying glass that appears when you click **add online video** in PowerPoint. Before you add the video, you will be able to preview it. Simply press **enter**, and it will appear in the currently selected slide.

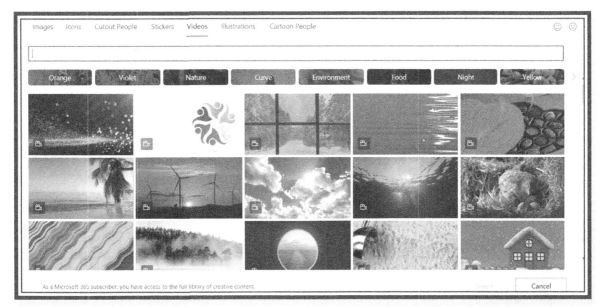

Stock Videos

Online Videos

In both the presentation and editing modes of the presentation, a **play button** will appear to play the video. You can also choose which features to apply to the video by clicking on it and noticing that **the ribbon** changes to include an additional bar labeled **video tools.** Change the borders of the image, apply image corrections, and add effects using this bar.

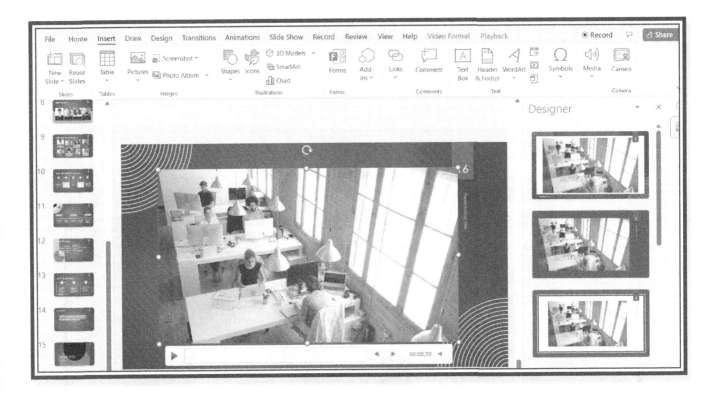

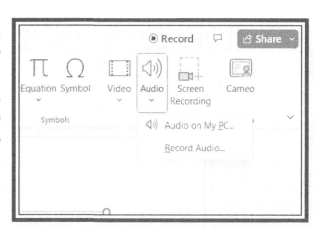

Sound will be added in a similar manner. In the **insert tab**, the button to add these media files is located next to the video button. You can add audio from your computer files or select a file using **record and audio** from your device. However, in order for the software to accept the function of recording your voice directly into the presentation, you must have the recording device connected and recognized.

Inserting Charts

Inserting charts and graphs into a presentation is simple, and the process is similar to doing so in Word. You will select the chart or graph you want to add, and the chart as well as an Excel file will open for you to enter the data.

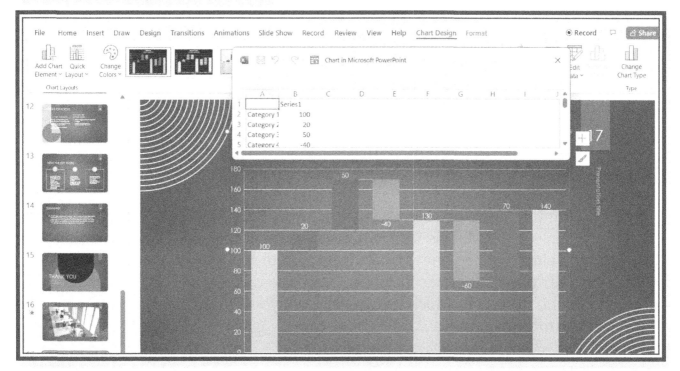

After adding the data, you can close the Excel window, and the chart will automatically refresh and update with the new information. If your graph is in Excel, you can also choose to copy and paste it to the presentation to avoid having to type in all of the information again.

Pro tip: *You can paste a graph from another program into Word or PowerPoint as a picture or as an interactive feature. When you paste a graph, the toolbox that appears immediately to the side of the graph will give you several options for how to paste it—as a picture, with links, or as a simple object.*

When you paste it as a picture, the elements do not move and remain the same. If you paste it with links, however, every time you modify the origin file, the chart will be modified as well, necessitating the opening of both programs so that the information can be updated once it is completed.

ANIMATING AND TRANSITIONING A PRESENTATION

If you've ever been to a presentation where the presenter used some nice special effects, you might be wondering how you can incorporate these into your own. These are useful for promoting an interactive feature of your presentation. While **transitions** describe the process of animating what happens to the slide when you switch from one to the other, **animations** describe what happens to the elements within the slide.

Inserting Transitions

When applying a transition to your slides, you can time them and choose whether or not they will have a sound. This tool is located in the transitions tab of the ribbon and allows you to select from a variety of transition methods. The first step is to determine which slide will receive the transition. In most cases, the slide that appears in your workspace will be the one to which it is applied, but you can choose another by selecting it from the **thumbnail panel.**

22°C Sunny   Search   09:00 AM 01/09/2023

Transitions Tab

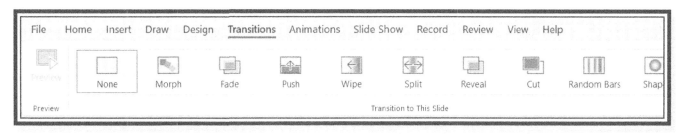

When you select an effect, it will initially display what it will look like when you present. To **preview** it multiple times, click the preview button on the far left of the ribbon.

The **timing section** is located to the far right of the same tab, where **you can specify how long you want this transition** between slides to last and whether or not you want a specific sound to play. PowerPoint has a set of default sounds that you can use, or you can select another one of your options by clicking on the drop-down arrow.

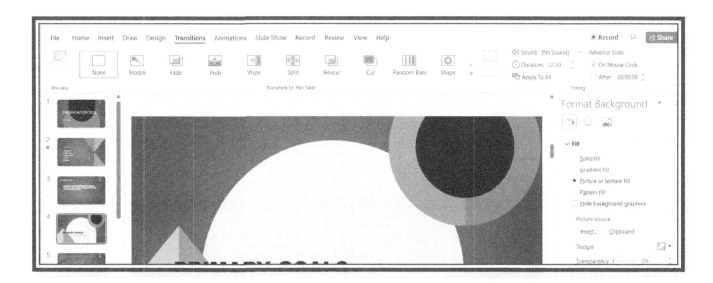

Finally, to round out the transition options, you can have the slide move to the next one with a **mouse click** or after a predetermined amount of time. The first option is ideal for those who want to control the presentation and what is displayed while they speak. The second option is best suited for recorded presentations, as we will see in the following section. It will allow others to read your presentation without the need for them to click to change the slide.

Inserting Animations

Adding animations to presentation elements is similar to adding a transition to the slide. Instead of inserting them into the entire slide, you can customize what happens to each part you present. This could be useful, for example, if you don't want your audience to be distracted by seeing all of the information at once.

To add an animation, navigate to the Animations tab in the ribbon. It will have a similar layout to the transitions tab and will contain many of the same features. To add an animation to an element, first select it by clicking on it and then choose the type of animation you want to use. You will also be able to determine **how long this will take and what the trigger will be, such as a mouse click.** You can, however, time the animations to appear at a specific time if you prefer.

Animations Tab

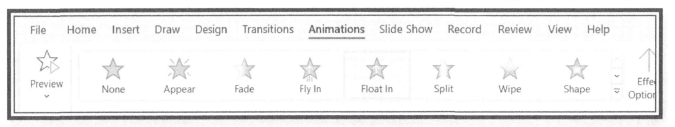

One of the best things about the animation feature is that you have access to a facilitator called the animation pane because you may have to manage so many of them in one slide.

This will show all of the features you've added to this slide on the right side of your work area. You can determine the order in which each animation will occur, whether they will transition to each other with or without a specific trigger, how long they will take, and play them all to see how your slide will look. This is also available in the **preview button** on the far left of the ribbon.

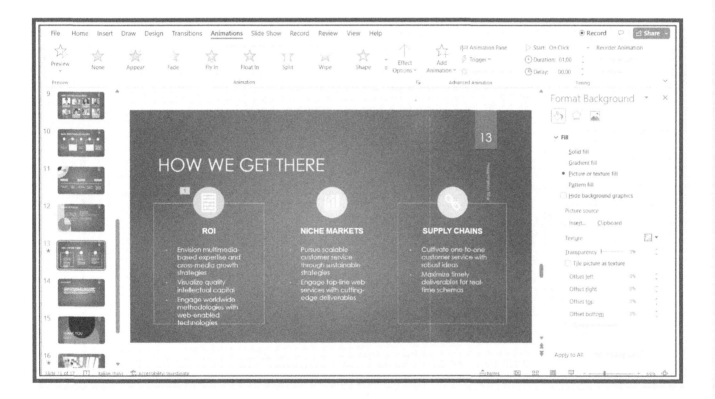

COMMENTS AND NOTES

When planning a presentation, make some notes about what you want to say while speaking. You can accomplish this by making notes on the slide you're working on. To add a **note** that only you will see during the presentation, **click on the click to add notes** box at the bottom of the slide. Whatever you add will be visible on your presentation screen and may be useful in helping you remember important topics to cover.

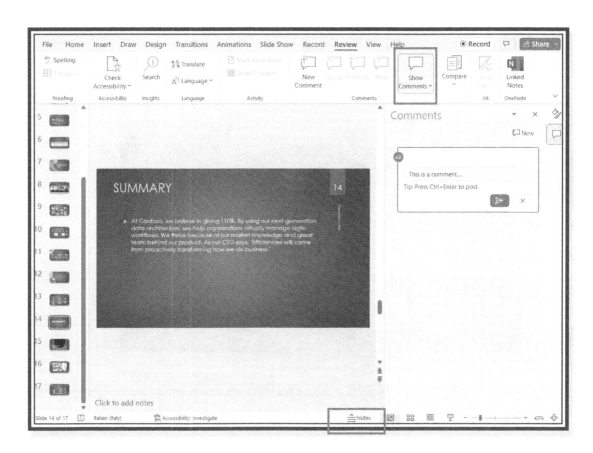

If you send this presentation to another person, you can also add a comment to the slide to include information that was not included in the file. To add one, go to the **review tab** in the ribbon and click the **add comment button**. To see all of the comments in the file, select the **show comments tab**, and they will all appear with the relevant slide displayed when you click on the relevant comment. These will not be visible during the presentation and will not appear in it.

HOW TO PRESENT AND PRINT

Now that your presentation is finished, you may be wondering, "What should I do to visualize how it will look?" PowerPoint includes a feature that allows you to view the final result. On the bottom right-hand corner of your screen, there are four options to the left of the zoom bar. They are as follows: **working view, layout view, reading view, and presentation view.**

The first option is the one we've been using so far, and it's the best one for editing and working on your presentation.

The second allows you to see the thumbnail image of every slide in your presentation outside of the thumbnail panel.

This feature is known as the **slide sorter,** and it allows you to move slides around but not change their content.

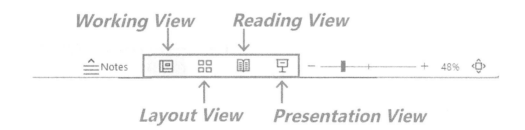

Following that is the **reading view**, which allows you to see how the presentation will appear to the viewer.

The final and most important view is the **presentation view**. When you select this option, you will see a minimized version of the current slide, a preview of the next slide, and the notes you have added. This is only useful if you are presenting from a computer or device that can display this information. If you are standing, for example, and do not have access to a computer to see what happens next, this view may be less useful.

Printing

Assume you want to **print** your presentation and see how it looks on paper. You can do it as well, and in a variety of ways. You can select the format for printing by clicking on the print function in the file tab. If you are giving a presentation to a client or in a course, you can choose to print one slide per page.

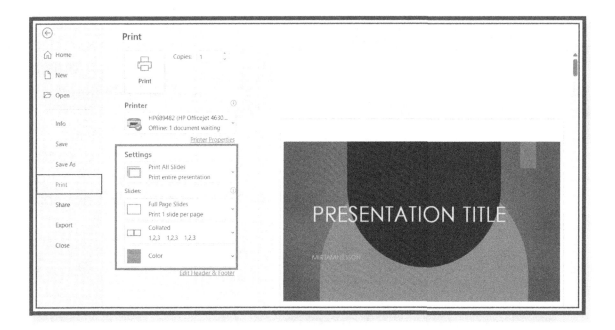

Another option is to print **notes pages** where there will be one slide at the top of the page and several lines to write on at the bottom. You can also choose to print only the presentation **outline**, which will filter your headings and titles to the file and will only print those.

Finally, if you want to save printing space and paper, you can print more than one slide on one page.

PowerPoint allows you to use up to nine slides per page, and you can select the orientation you want in the third box of the settings tool, which says **print only one sided.**

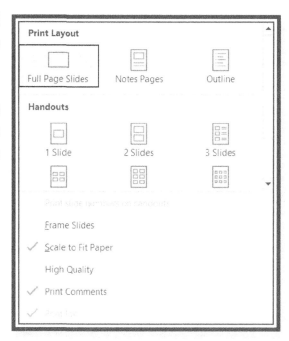

RECORDING A PRESENTATION

Last but not least, you should become acquainted with the **recording feature** that PowerPoint has made available to its users. If you are a teacher, for example, and want to give an automated class into which you have prerecorded your voice, this tool will come in handy. It could also be an online course that you intend to publish on the internet and distribute to other users.

The **record** feature is accessible via the ribbon's record tab. You can choose whether to begin recording from a specific slide or to begin recording from the beginning. Once the recording is complete, you can add your own audio to it (for example, a narration or a song), and then export it to video. The software will allow you to save in the format you believe is best for sharing with those who have access to it..

Record Tab

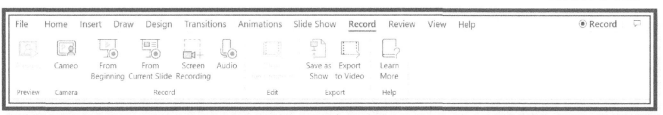

KEYBOARD SHORTCUTS

FUNCTION	SHORTCUT ON PC	SHORTCUT ON MAC
Start a presentation	F5	Command + Shift + Return
Show presenter view	Alt + F5	Option + Return
Close presenter view	Esc	Esc
Move slide during presentation	Arrows or enter	Arrows or return
Go to last slide	End	End
Go to first slide	Home	Home
Go to next slide	Page down	Not available
Go to previous slide	Page up	Not available
Hide pointer and navigation	Ctrl + H	Not available
View computer taskbar	Ctrl + T	Not available
Add new slide	Ctrl + M	Command + Shift + N
Open Zoom dialogue box	Alt + W, Q	Command + (+) or (-)
Open recording feature	Alt + C	Not available
Expand or collapse the ribbon	Ctrl + F1	Command + F1
Select all objects in a slide	Ctrl + A	Command + A
Copy animation painter	Alt + Shift + C	Not available
Insert a text box	Alt + N, X	Not available
Insert WordArt	Alt + N, W	Not available
Group a selected group	Ctrl + G	Command + Option + G
Expand all groups	Alt + Shift + 9	Not available

Section 4:
Microsoft ACCESS

Despite the prevalent lack of proficiency among individuals in utilizing the Microsoft Access software within the suite, it is indeed regarded as one of the most effective tools for constructing an information database. Although users have the option to create a document from scratch, the program provides multiple templates that can be used as a starting point for their work. These functionalities encompass the ability to establish a comprehensive repository of contacts, maintain a ledger, facilitate project management, oversee task allocation, and provide customer service, among a multitude of other features. This tool exhibits particular efficacy for businesses lacking proprietary software for managing their daily operations, necessitating a swift and dependable system for this purpose.

LET'S START WITH THE BASICS

Access has a ribbon that enables the user to perform the majority of the functions, as you might have inferred from previous chapters, and Excel is the program that Access is most similar to. It is safe to say that if you are familiar with some of Excel's tools, you will

22°C
Sunny

Search

W X P A O S T N P

09:00 AM
01/09/202

be able to work with Access, especially if you are proficient with the pivot table function.

All of the options on the **Access ribbon—create, external data, and database tools**—are associated with databases. The system will let you filter, create reports, edit, and even import data from other files you might have on your computer after you've created your own file. The text formatting features of the program are less crucial in this case because we are discussing a control tool. In any case, they are accessible for those who want to format their documents using the same style as what we have seen in other chapters in the home tab of the ribbon.

Home tab

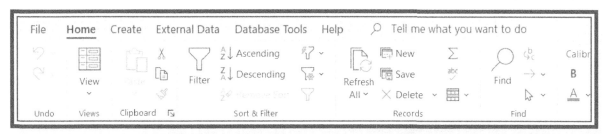

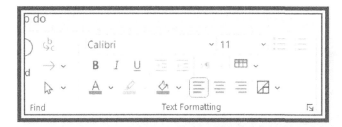

CREATING A NEW DATABASE

A new database can be created when you launch Access for the first time or from the file tab in the ribbon, just like it can with the other programs you have already read about in this book. Options ranging from an empty database where you can start from scratch to templates that Microsoft has already formatted will be among the options that will appear. The requirement to name your database before working on it, in contrast to other programs where you can choose to name the file after starting the file, is one of the distinctions you'll notice here.

22°C
Sunny
🔍 Search

09:00 AM
01/09/2023
127

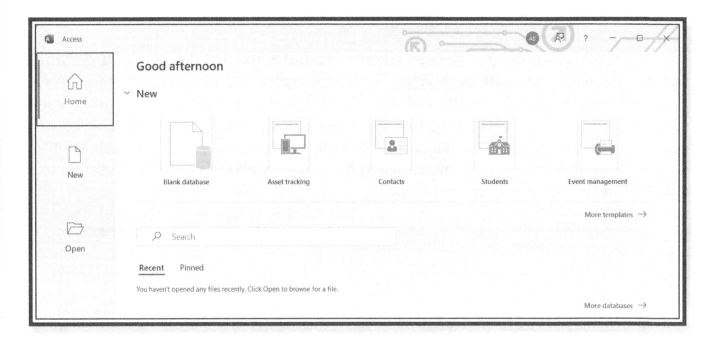

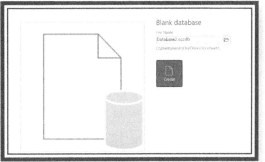

We will concentrate on building a new database from scratch because the procedures for using Access' templates are fairly simple. When you select this option, a straightforward table with rows and columns and no named fields will appear.

The first thing to understand is that if you don't fill out the existing lines in the tables, Access won't let you add more. For instance, a second line will appear for you to add the information after you complete the first line of the table.

Renaming Fields

You might need to rename the fields for each column depending on your needs because the blank database comes with standard names and data. Double clicking on the names of the columns will make them editable, so do that first. The same will apply to any fields you've already filled out with data. You can edit the data in a cell by double clicking on it, which causes it to automatically highlight and become highlighted.

22°C
Sunny

Search

09:00 AI
01/09/202

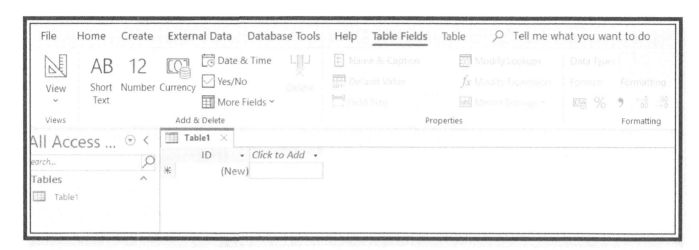

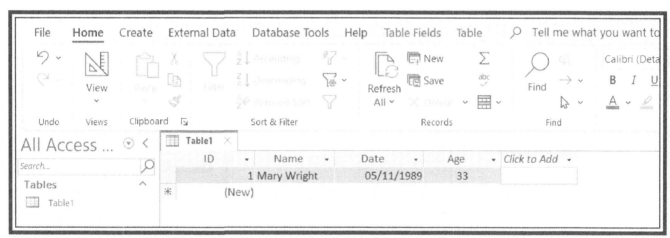

Pro tip: *Additionally, you will only be able to add new columns to your datasheet once you have decided on the names of the ones that already exist. When you've finished, your work area will automatically include the option to add a new column.*

How to Filter and Sort

As soon as you have entered the pertinent data into the table, Access will enable you to filter it in the manner of your choice. You will be able to sort your data alphabetically or numerically in either ascending or descending order in addition to filtering it according to your data.

You will quickly recognize these features if you recall our lesson from the Excel chapter because they function similarly. Although the report will also present you with this information in a grouped manner, doing so may make it easier for you to visualize the data.

Home tab

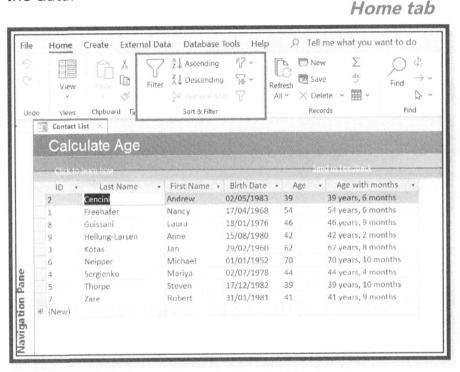

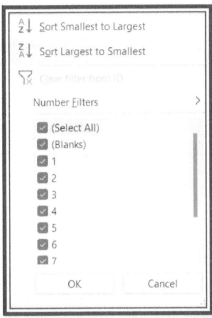

Learn Other Functionalities

Access has a number of other options for creating files with media, dialogue boxes, check boxes, a blank form, and other features, even though its primary function is to store data. By selecting the appropriate button—application parts or blank form—under **the create tab in the ribbon**, you can add them. With the help of all this information, the data can be mapped in a database so that it can be analyzed after being added. Others will be able to add data to the database without having to see all of its content or standardize what the input will be by using the features of application parts or blank forms.

Access also has functions like **finding and replacing, adding equations, and spell checking**. We won't go over these again since we did so in the earlier chapters. However, as they apply to all Microsoft Suite softwares, please refer to them if you have any questions about how they operate.

ADDING TABLES

Since managing Access is its main purpose, **adding tables** will be its most crucial feature. When you add a table, you'll notice that Table 2 is listed as a tab at the top of the work area. Let's say you want to give these tables a new name to make them easier to remember. You must use the right button to click on the **navigation pane** to the left of the workspace to access it. You can select what you want to do with this table from a drop-down menu, **including deleting, renaming, and viewing the table's properties.**

Create tab

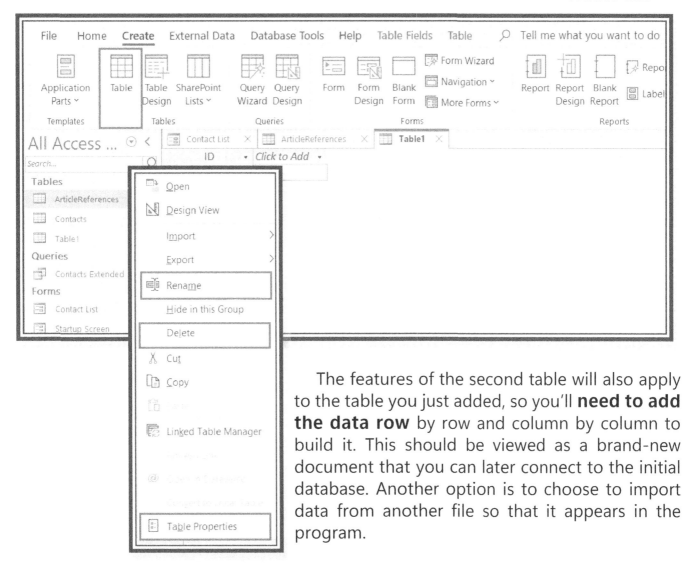

The features of the second table will also apply to the table you just added, so you'll **need to add the data row** by row and column by column to build it. This should be viewed as a brand-new document that you can later connect to the initial database. Another option is to choose to import data from another file so that it appears in the program.

You must click the new data source button under the external data tab in the ribbon to accomplish this. Following that, you can choose whether to add a file from your computer, an online source, another database, or other sources.

External Data tab

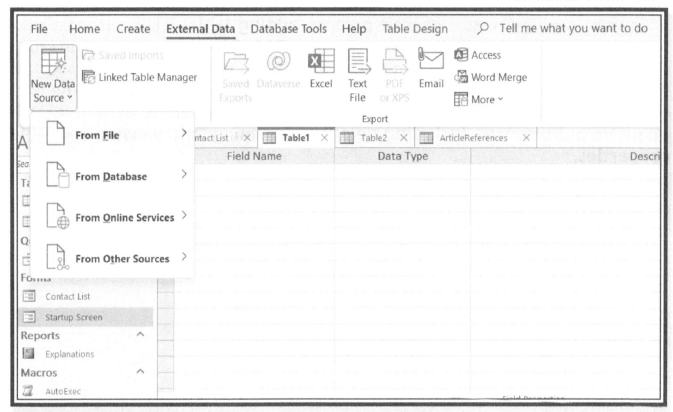

Access will present you with the options to import the data to **a new database, add it to an existing database, or create a table maintaining the link to Excel once you have decided what type of file you want to upload.** In the final scenario, if you decide to create the link, the database will be updated each time you change the original file. If it does not do so automatically, you can refresh the page by clicking the refresh button found in the ribbon's home tab.

> *Pro tip: The table name tabs may not be used right away or they may not be needed at all when they are placed on top of the workspace. The information won't be lost if you click the x button to close them. To see the table in your workspace once more, click on its name in the l**eft pane.***

22°C
Sunny

Search

09:00 AM
01/09/202

Formatting Fields

You might not need to manually configure the table as you would in other software, which is one of Access' best features. You can set the column or field you want to be **short text, number, currency, date and time, or yes and no check boxes** with just a few clicks on its quick tools. If none of these fit your requirements, you can also use the **more fields button,** which has an arrow pointing downward next to it and will bring you to a list of additional, less precise options.

Table Fields tab

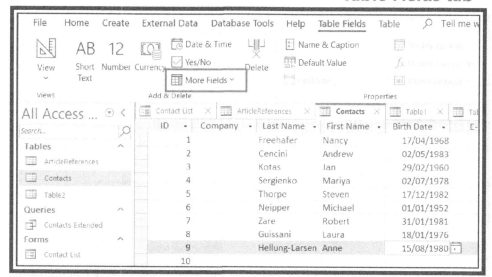

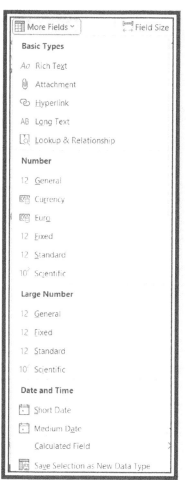

Some of the options that this tool will automatically provide to configure your table include **addresses**, where all pertinent fields will be added to the table; payment type, which provides you with a number of payment options as well as a data validation menu; or even a **status bar,** which enables you to set the project's progress, for instance. These are just a few of the options available to you that will help you better organize and set up your database.

Pro tip: The quick formatting buttons will automatically add new fields rather than replacing existing ones when adding new fields to the database. Remember to always set the cursor to the last available column so that this information is inserted to the end or to have it on the column before where you want the new data to be placed in order to prevent your table from being incorrectly configured as a result of adding a field in the middle of your information.

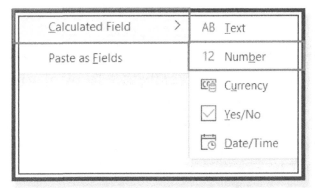

The option to use calculated fields is the last formatting tool available in Access. These will enable you to apply to your database the same functionality as an Excel spreadsheet.

When you click on the column's header, the table fields tab will appear on the ribbon, allowing you to add one of these fields. The next step is to select more fields, and the last choice is to **add a calculated field**. Choose the option that you want to use. A number is one example.

You can choose the calculation you want to use by selecting it in a dialogue box that will open. The fields you want to calculate can now be selected and entered in the text box. The calculated item **([field 1] + [field 2] + [field 3])/3** is an illustration. Access will compute the data automatically and compute the average of the fields you've chosen.

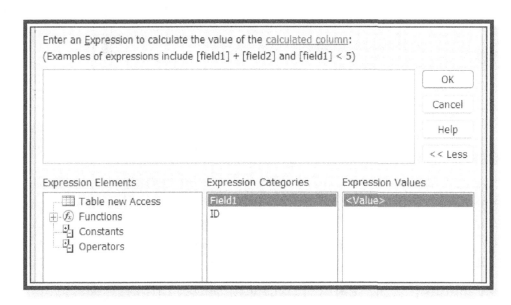

Pro tip: *Keep in mind that the formatting of these fields will depend on the kind of function you want to run. They would all need to be number fields in the example above so that they could be calculated properly.*

22°C
Sunny

🔍 Search

09:00 AM
01/09/202

Visualizing and Moving Fields

You can move your column using the **drag and drop** options provided by Access, even if you unintentionally misplace it. Click on the field's title with the cursor to select it. A black line will then appear to the field's left. This line will specify the location of the column. You can decide where to leave it based on your needs and preferences.

> **Pro tip:** Similar to how you would in Excel, manually determine the width of your columns and lines.

You can also access a drop-down menu with a number of options by clicking on the column's title with the right mouse button on your computer.

These consist of inserting fields, **hiding or revealing fields,** copying and pasting content into columns, and even freezing the pertinent column. If you need to scroll through a table with many columns in order to view the information, the **freezing option is especially useful.**

Consider a scenario in which you are working with a student list from a school and you need to produce a report on their grades. One student

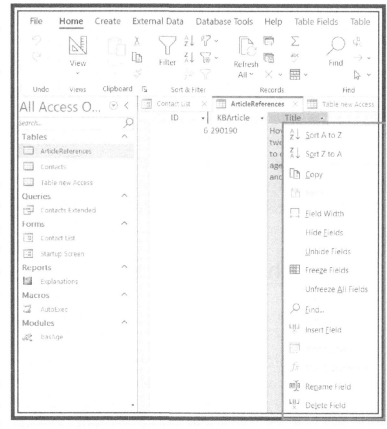

would be represented by each line, and their class would be represented by each column. Your goal is to compile a database of all the grades that 9th graders have earned. Even if the teacher's reports are all in the same alphabetical order, it helps to have a point of reference for the student's name as you scroll through the 20+ columns so that you don't miss anything.

In this scenario, you would select freeze fields from the right-click menu after moving to the names-containing column. By doing this, the column will move automatically to the database's first column and the names of the students will always be visible as you scroll sideways. In contrast to Excel, **you can select to freeze individual columns in Access**, and the data will be presented in the order you have chosen. Go back to the drop-down menu with the right button and select Unfreeze Fields to return to the standard visualization.

> **Pro tip:** *All of the frozen fields will be reset to their original positions once you unfreeze them. After working on the pertinent information, you will need to manually move the cells back to their original positions if you want to change the order.*

RELATIONS AND QUERIES

The two most important tools in Access are **relations and queries**; these are essentially what set it apart from Excel. These enable you to generate reports later on, conduct quick searches, and create connections between the data you have added to your database. Let's examine each of their respective roles.

Establishing Relations

We should return to your example of the students and the grades to illustrate the significance of establishing relationships in Access. Consider that after making a table with all of their grades, you now want to make another table with their personal data. You'll make a table, and it's critical that it share at least one field with the first table. It is possible to accomplish this by creating a student ID number or perhaps by using their first and last names. It will all depend on your preferences, but always choosing to give the database a special ID number is the best choice. To make it simpler to identify the student, keep in mind that this information must be specific to them.

Then, you will **create a new database** and populate it with all the pertinent details about their personal information, including their address, phone number, name of their teacher, and any other information you deem pertinent. You must now select the relationships button under the database tools tab of the ribbon in order to create the

22°C
Sunny

Search W X P A O S T N P

09:00 AM
01/09/202

relationship between the two tables. With a pane on the right listing every table in your database, this will open a new view in your workspace.

Database Tools Tab

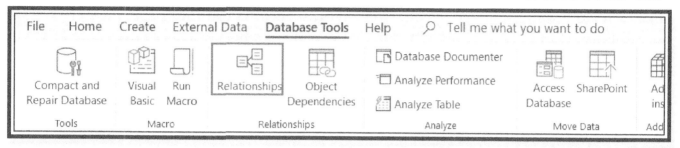

To access the work view, double click on the table's name. As soon as you do, a fresh box will appear, each of which has a name and a key next to it. These show what your table's primary key is. Drag the appropriate name to the one in the other box to establish their connection. When you do this, Access will ask you to specify their relationship in a new dialogue box that appears.

Relationships Design Tab

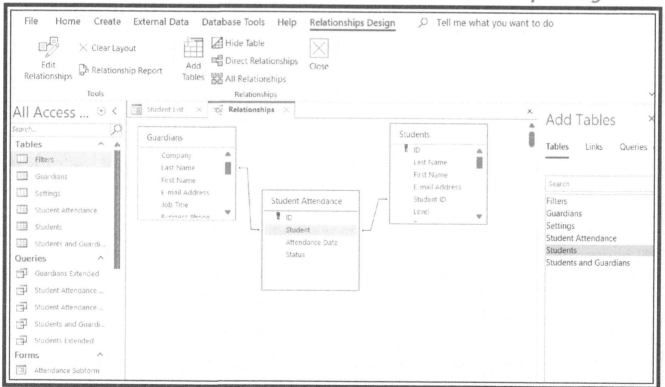

You're all set once you've completed this! You can work with both tables simultaneously because the relationship between them has been established. The software will ask you if you want to save the relationship when you click the x on the relationship tab. It should have a name and be saved. When you return to the database view after doing so, a relationship table option with the name you specified will show up in the left hand pane.

Queries

You can filter the data in your database using **queries**, using the information you already have. Using this tool, you can create some extremely complex queries that might aid in helping you visualize the data in accordance with your needs. You'll need to select the **create tab** from the ribbon in order to create a query. This option will be accessible in the queries section, where you can create queries with the **wizard's assistance** or independently using query design.

Create Tab

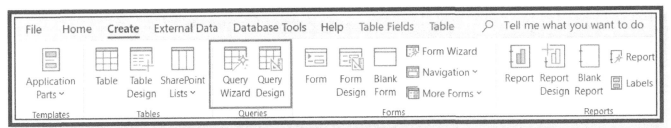

Let's use the students and their grades as an example for this chapter. Let's say that after entering all the necessary details and creating the necessary connections, you now want to view all of the people who received a math grade lower than 80%. The **new query button** will be the first thing you should click. Once more, the workspace will appear differently to you, and the left pane containing the names of the tables will once more be visible. Double-click on the names of the tables you want to use to select them, or drag and drop them onto the workspace. They will also be noted if there is a relationship between these tables. It is the student **ID number** in our situation.

Double-click on the table box containing the fields you want to include in your query to select them. As you proceed, you'll notice that they'll appear in the same order in the table below the workspace. You can decide what will happen to the fields after you have chosen all of the pertinent ones to include in the query. As was already mentioned, we

22°C Sunny Search W X P A O S T N P 09:00 AM 01/09/202 only want students whose math grades are lower than 80% to show up. As a result, we will select the column containing this data and t**ype =>80% in the criteria line**.

Query Wizard

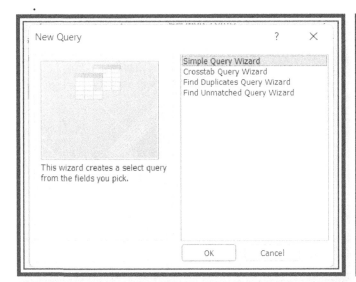

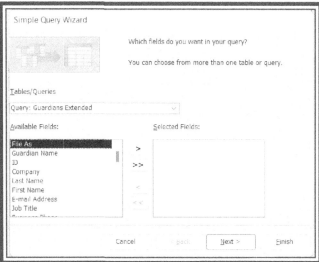

When finished, save the query and give it a new name (you can also do this by clicking the x button on the tab). The query will have the same effect as the relationships did in the left-hand pane. Your query is finished when you see all of the students who meet this requirement in your workspace view. According to the criteria you require, you can create as many queries as you like. For each subject where the students have a grade below 80%, for instance, you could create a single query.

Query

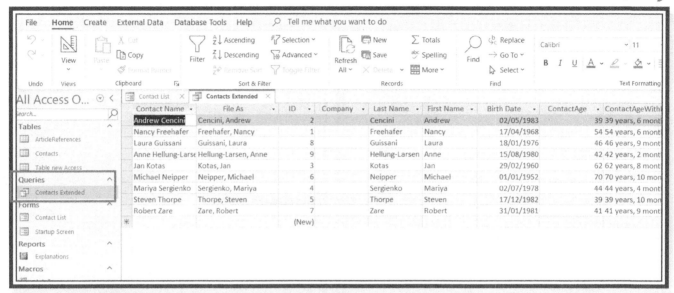

CREATING REPORTS

How to create reports is the final crucial aspect of Access that you need to understand. You've already built the databases you want, built the connections, and now you need to produce reports based on this data. Given that the previous steps completed all of the difficult work, this is the final and most straightforward step. The reports also give the user access to some very innovative features, such as the ability to choose a style and an aesthetic. You can either make your own style or use one of the predetermined ones the software offers for this.

Let's say you want to create a report card with the students' grades, using our example of their grades one last time. These must include their names, contact information, course information, and grades. You must select the report button under the create tab in the ribbon in order to create a report. A new window will open, and the ribbon will reveal a toolbar for report design layout.

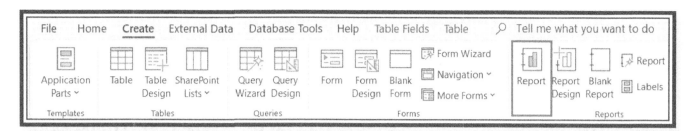

Pro tip: You have a report wizard that will help you create the report to meet your needs, just like most of the other features in Access. You can use this tool to define the best approach for your report if you are unsure of how it will appear once you are finished.

Report Layout Deisgn Tab

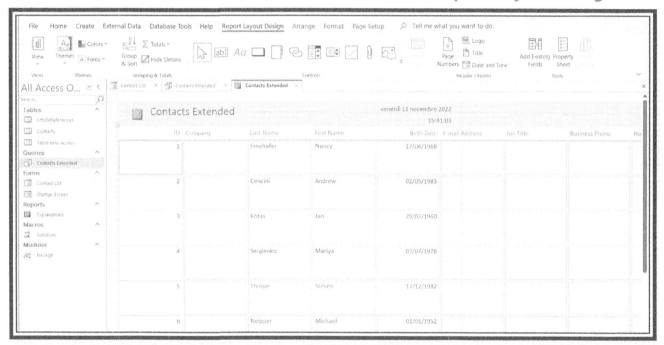

Here, you can select the details you want included in the report based on your requirements. This report gives you the option of including your logo, a title, page numbers, and even an image. After choosing every field that will be available, simply click the x to close the view, save it with the name of your choice, and you're done! This report will once more be visible in the program's left hand pane. To determine whether the report satisfies your needs, **use the print preview option**.

KEYBOARD SHORTCUTS

FUNCTION	SHORTCUT ON PC	SHORTCUT ON MAC
Go to home tab	Ctrl + H	Command + H
Open existing database	Ctrl + O	Command + O
Switch views of database	F5	Not available
Switch from edit to view mode	F2	Not available
Move to other datasheet view	Tab key or Shift + Tab	Tab key
Exit Access	Alt + F4	Not available
Go to create tab	Alt + C	Not available
Go to table tab	Alt + J, T	Not available
Go to database tools tab	Alt+Y, 2	Not available
Go to external data tab	Alt + X	Not available
Show or hide property sheet	F4	Not available
Move to beginning of entry	Home	Home
Move to end of entry	End	End
Move between lines	Arrow keys	Arrow keys
Move to next field	Tab key	Tab key
Move to previous field	Shift + Tab	Not available
Select a column	Shift + arrow key	Shift + arrow key
Remove the selected column	Spacebar or (-) sign	Not available

 22°C Sunny 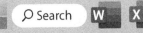 Search W X P A O S T N P  09:00 AM 01/09/202

Section 5: Microsoft OUTLOOK

Email correspondence is widely recognized as a prevalent mode of communication in contemporary times. To facilitate this process, Microsoft offers a dedicated application for email management as part of its suite, namely **Microsoft Outlook**. In contrast to other applications, the utilization of this software necessitates the establishment of an appropriately configured user account.

LET'S START BY SETUP YOUR ACCOUNT

For those with personal emails who have accounts on services like Gmail, Yahoo, or Hotmail, we'll use the most typical example because there are several ways to set up an account in Outlook. A welcome screen with instructions will appear when you first launch the program. If it's not the first time, you'll need to manually search for the appropriate location.

First, select account settings from the file tab of the ribbon. You should navigate to the first tab, labeled "Email," in the dialogue box that will open. To add your account, click the new button, which has a tiny envelope on it, there. Then you should enter your

address in the new box that will appear. Next, click the connect button and enter the necessary data the system requires, including your name, email address, and password. When finished, press the following button. Your password might need to be entered once more. Otherwise, press finish, and your account will be created.

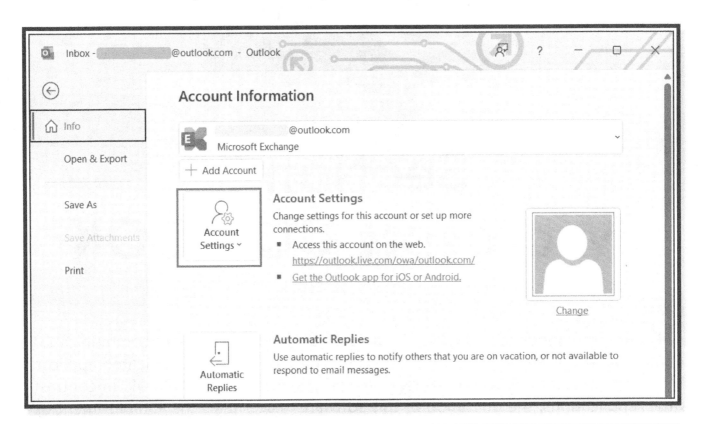

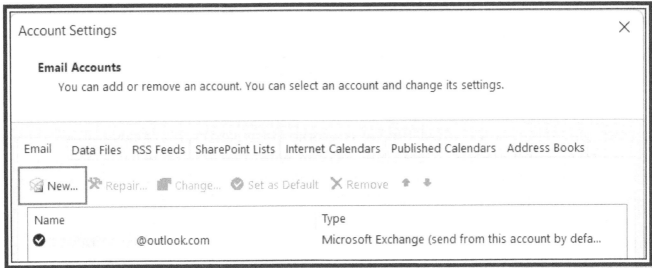

When you are finished, you will be directed to your **inbox**, where you can manage and view all of your messages. The majority of the message-related features are accessible from the **home tab** of the ribbon. In actuality, there are only four tabs on the Outlook ribbon, excluding the help and file ones.

Home Tab

Setting a Signature

When using Outlook, one of the main tasks a user will want to complete is creating a signature. Open a **new message** to start one. Although you won't always be typing one, it will allow you to choose the **signature** you want to use. The option signature is located in the **include section** of the **message tab** of the ribbon once the message has been opened. Select **signatures** by clicking the button. You should see a new dialogue box appear where you can enter the desired information.

To begin a **new signature** and give it a name, select new. In the event that you decide against adding signatures automatically, this name will show up in the drop-down menu. You should enter your desired signoff for your messages in the bottom box—the biggest of all—where it says **edit signature.** Font, color, and other style information that is shared by other Suite applications can be formatted here.

You can then decide under what circumstances this signature will appear after you're finished. If you have more than one signature, **you can choose which one to use by selecting the option for default signature in the right-hand menu.** In this section, you can designate a signature for each email account you want to add, decide which one to use for new messages, and decide which one to use for **replies and forwards.**

Despite having a signature set, you have the option of leaving these fields empty and only adding the signature to the messages you choose. You must set the signature and click "OK" without configuring these features in order to accomplish this. You can return to the signature button whenever you are getting ready to send a message and choose the one you want to use for that particular message.

CREATING AND SENDING EMAILS

In order to create a signature, you have already seen how to begin a new message. By selecting the **new email button**, you can access this function. You type your message into the message box that will then appear. You can format it however you like by using the text formatting tools in the ribbon, but keep in mind that not all recipients may be able to see the formatting. Their viewing capabilities and the program they have will determine this.

The **bcc (blind carbon copy)** is not automatically added; you must manually add it. The message's to and **cc (carbon copy)** are readily available. To do this, click the to or cc buttons to bring up a dialogue box with the bcc option. Enter just one address, then **click "OK"** to proceed. Going to the options tab in the ribbon and selecting the options bcc and from under the **show fields section** are other ways to make the **bcc field visible.** To view the referred field and make any desired changes to what you can see, click on each of these buttons.

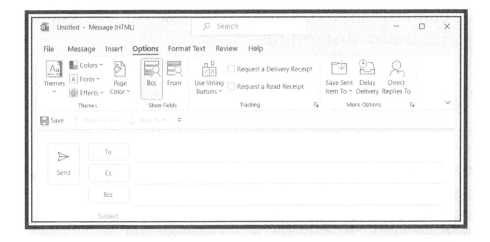

22°C Sunny

09:00 AM
01/09/202

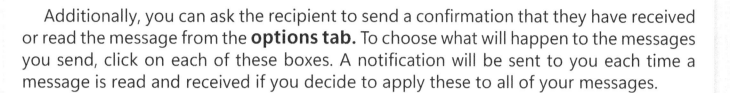
Additionally, you can ask the recipient to send a confirmation that they have received or read the message from the **options tab.** To choose what will happen to the messages you send, click on each of these boxes. A notification will be sent to you each time a message is read and received if you decide to apply these to all of your messages.

Delayed Delivery

You may choose, for example, to have a message delivered the following morning when sending it if you don't want it to arrive right away. The configuration of the message can also be set up to accomplish this. You can choose to use the **delay delivery option** in the more options section of the **options tab**. A dialogue box will open after you select this choice, allowing you to enter the necessary details. You can choose when you want the message to be delivered, who you want to receive the responses from, and how long you want the message to last before it expires.

Options Tab

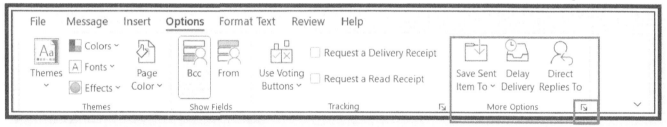

Delivery Options

Determining Importance for each E-mail

The ability to assign a message a **high or low priority** is one of the features that come with Outlook. You can do this by clicking on the **exclamation point** to set a high priority or the **blue arrow** pointing down to set a **low priority for emails.**

Message Tab

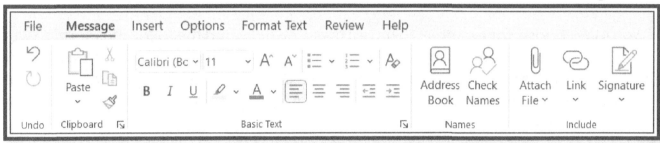

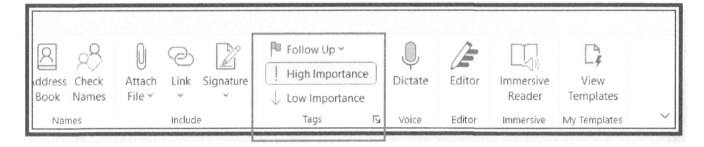

By clicking on the red flag, you can also determine whether the message needs to be followed up on.

When you do, a drop-down menu will appear, allowing you to specify the time frame for the program's follow-up reminder. Although the program gives you a few standard options to choose from, you can also create your own reminder by changing the date.

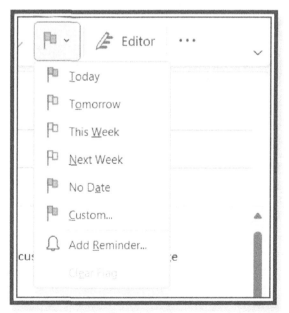

22°C
Sunny
Search
09:00 AM
01/09/202

Polling Through Email

We occasionally email groups of people to get their approval on a project. Did you know that Outlook has a **polling tool** you can use to get answers sent to you? Additionally, you can specify this while writing the message in the **options tab.**

Options Tab

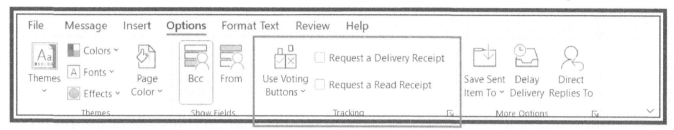

There will be a button labeled **"use voting buttons"** in the **tracking options.** The recipients of the message can choose between **accepting or rejecting the message as well as between yes, no, and maybe by clicking on it,** which will open a drop-down menu. You can also add your own customizations to these buttons in the dialogue box by separating the available choices with a semicolon.

Adding Attachments and Images

Did you know that images and pictures can be included in message body instead of as an attachment? But once more, it's crucial to be aware that not everyone may receive it as a message but as an attachment. This will depend on how they are set up. Use the features on the ribbon to make the appropriate additions; they'll function similarly to what we saw in the earlier chapters.

However, the size that your service provider permits will determine whether you can add an attachment. **For instance, Gmail only permits attachments up to 5GB in size.** By selecting the attach file button, which is present on both the home and insert tabs of the ribbon, you can **include the file(s) in the message if they fall within the permitted range.** When you click the button, a list of the most recent files you've opened will appear, or you can browse your computer to find more.

CHAPTER 5

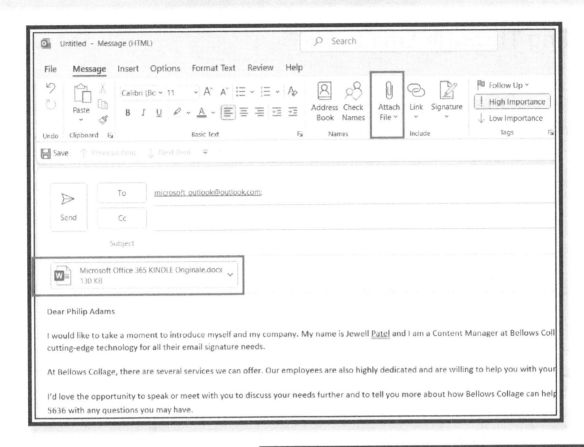

There are two additional ways to send files with your message. Drag and drop the file(s) into the message window as a first step. By doing this, the file will be automatically inserted into the message you will send.

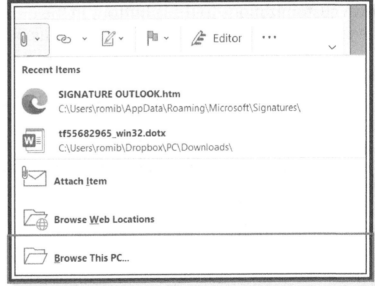

Copying and pasting files into the message window is the alternative method of adding files. You can send files to the recipient using either method, and both are acceptable.

Pro tip: *Simply click on the files you have attached and press the delete key on your keyboard to remove them. They will be automatically deleted as a result, and if you decide to put them back, they must be attached once more.*

Automatic Out-of-Office Messages

An automatic reply that recipients will see if you are temporarily unavailable to read your emails is one of the most practical features to have. These, also referred to as a "out of office message," will be set up so that whenever you leave the office, for example, to go on vacation, people will be alerted and informed that they cannot reach you, that you cannot access your messages, or any other message that you would like to convey.

You must select the **automatic replies (out of office)** option under account information on the file tab in order to apply the message. When you get there, you can choose to **send automated responses.** Toggle this box. Setting a date is not necessary if the message is one that users will receive regardless of how they get in touch with you. However, select the only send during this time range option if you want to specify a **specific time frame** for when senders will receive this message.

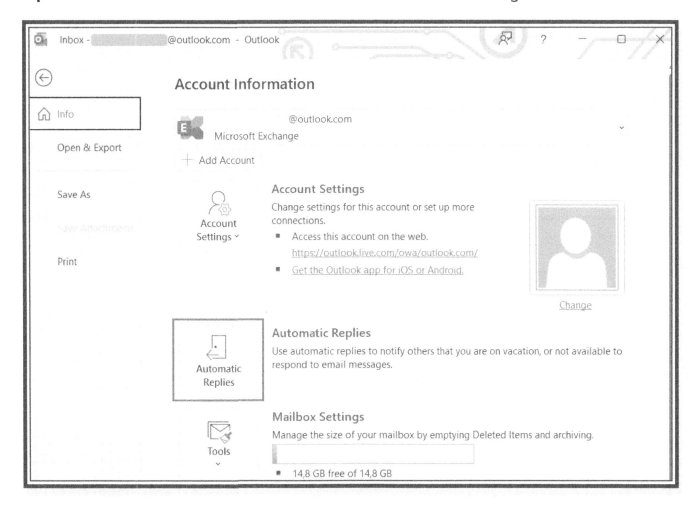

You can type the message and put your signature in the box that appears next. You will still be able to access your messages normally even though those who send you messages will receive these messages.

After you have finished writing your message, click "ok" to activate the feature.

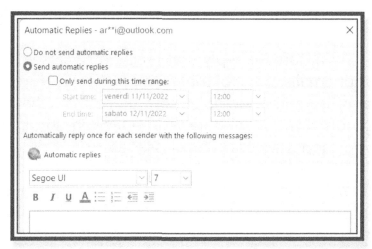

Pro tip: *When you open your Outlook page, a yellow banner will appear. If you want to turn off the out-of-office messages, click on it. You can either click the turn off button that will be there, or you can go to the file tab and click the turn off button in the automatic replies section.*

INBOX FOLDERS

If you don't **automatically file** your messages, they will show up in your inbox. You have the option of organizing your messages into **folders** or leaving them all in your inbox.

Home Tab

Selecting the inbox icon in the taskbar's left side and pressing the right button on it will **create a folder.** You must choose create new folder from the menu that will then appear. You can **drag and drop** the messages you want to place inside it into a folder that you can name according to your needs.

You can **search for messages** in your mailbox using the blue "search" bar at the top of the window. When you enter the search term there, Outlook will look through all of the relevant messages in the inbox and folders.

Search Bar

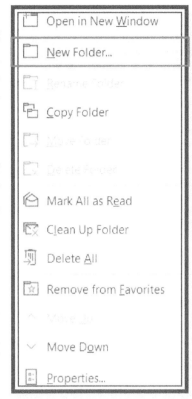

> **Pro tip:** *The entire contents of your email box will be searched for if you conduct a search while Outlook is on the inbox page. However, the program will only look for emails that are located in the same folder if you are already inside of it.*

CONTACTS

You can easily **create contacts** within your Outlook inbox, which will help you send emails faster. For the contacts you choose to add, the software has a section specifically for creating what they refer to as **business cards.** You must click on the icon with two people on it at the left-hand bottom of the taskbar to access this software feature.

The contacts section of Outlook will open once you click on it. Here, you can decide whether to create a **single contact** or a collection of contacts. Click on the **new contact button** in the home tab, which is located on the far left of the ribbon, **to add a new contact.** When you have finished, it will appear in the contacts section. A new window will open where you can fill out all the necessary information.

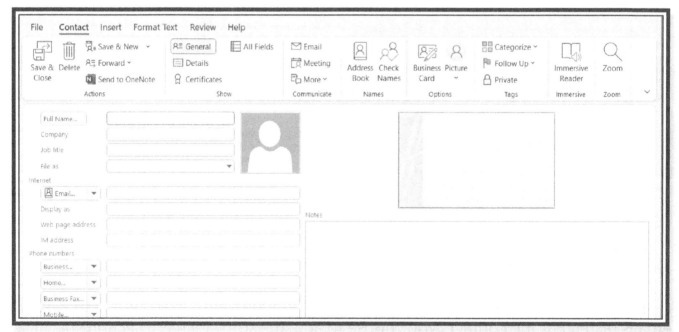

Contact Information

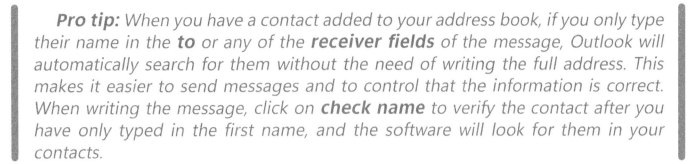

Pro tip: *When you have a contact added to your address book, if you only type their name in the* **to** *or any of the* **receiver fields** *of the message, Outlook will automatically search for them without the need of writing the full address. This makes it easier to send messages and to control that the information is correct. When writing the message, click on* **check name** *to verify the contact after you have only typed in the first name, and the software will look for them in your contacts.*

CALENDAR

The calendar is another tool offered by Outlook to the user for scheduling appointments and meetings. It also has a quick shortcut for inviting **guests to events or registering for meetings.** The calendar-like icon located at the bottom of the task panel can also be used to access this area of Outlook. When you do, a window with a calendar-like layout will appear. You can scroll through this page to see your upcoming appointments by day, week, or month. To choose the calendar view you want, use the **arrange feature on the home tab of the ribbon.**

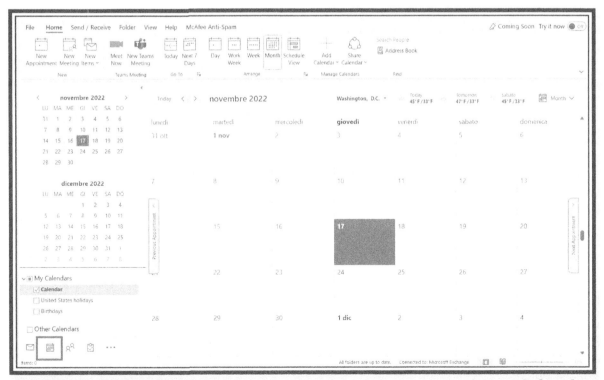

Calendar

Scheduling an Appointment or a Meeting

Double click on the date you want to book an **appointment or a meeting** in order to start it right away on your calendar. When you do, a new window with the option to enter the event's specifics will appear. Write a title that will appear as the author's name in the calendar. Additionally, you can choose whether the event will **last all day or just have a start and end time.** To ensure that the right time is set when working with teams from different time zones, check the time zones box.

Pro tip: If you have **Microsoft Teams** installed on your computer (more on this will be covered in Chapter 7), you can click the **Team Meeting** icon to automatically add a link to your appointment, which will send it to all attendees and give them access to it for the meeting.

By selecting the recurring button, you can specify the days on which the event will repeat itself, as in the case of a recurring training schedule. The features that are available on the ribbon can also be used to set up additional features, such as the reminder, the significance of the meeting, and how your day will appear in the calendar.

TASKS

You can **create tasks** in Outlook that you can then follow up on as necessary. An icon of a flag is used to represent this tool. You can activate the **flags in the tags** section of the home tab in the ribbon if you have an email that you want to mark for later follow-up. Once you click the button, you'll be given the option to **select the time you want to be reminded of this task.** These should be used for emails that require an attachment and that you want to keep track of.

Click on the clipboard with a checkmark at the base of the inbox pane to view all of your outstanding tasks. It will then display your current tasks and to-do list.

Eliminate the flag by clicking on the message with your right mouse button to remove a task from your list. You can choose to either mark the task as complete or to delete it for this. Pick the option that best suits your requirements.

Pro tip: There is a connection between Outlook and OneNote, as you will see in Chapter 9. Setting up tasks in OneNote and sending them to Outlook will be possible. You can also send something from Outlook to OneNote in the opposite direction. To do this, choose the item to send to a notebook and click the send to OneNote button on the home tab of the ribbon. Following your click, a dialogue box asking you which notebook you want to add the data you are exporting from Outlook to will appear. For more information on using the OneNote program, please see Chapter 9.

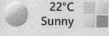

KEYBOARD SHORTCUTS

FUNCTION	SHORTCUT ON PC	SHORTCUT ON MAC
Close a window	Esc	Command + W
Create new message	Ctrl + Shift + M	Command + N (in mail window)
Send a message	Alt + S	Command + Return
Insert a file	Alt + N, A, F	Command + E
Search for an item	F3	Option + Command + F
Reply to a message	Alt +H, R, P	Command + R
Forward a message	Alt + H, F, W	Command + J
Reply all	Alt + H, R, A	Shift + Command + R
Check for new messages	Ctrl +M or F9	not available
Mail view	Ctrl +1	Command + 1
Calendar view	Ctrl + 2	Command + 2
Contacts view	Ctrl + 3	Command + 3
Tasks view	Ctrl + 4	Command + 4
Notes view	Ctrl + 5	Command + 5
Shortcuts	Ctrl + 7	Command + 7
Next open message	Ctrl + .	Command + ~
Previous open message	Ctrl + ,	Shift + Command + ~
Create appointment	Ctrl + Shift + A	Command + N
Create contact	Ctrl + Shift + C	Command + N
Create note	Ctrl + Shift + N	Command + N

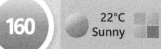

Section 6: Microsoft SKYPE

In contrast to the remaining applications featured in this publication, **Skype is a chat and messaging software that did not originate from Microsoft in its initial development stages.** In 2011, Microsoft acquired the aforementioned entity as a replacement for Microsoft Live Messenger, which had been introduced in 2003. Skype users have the capability to engage in voice calls, video calls, or text-based chats. The transmission of files and audio is facilitated as well. The aforementioned software can be downloaded by users onto various platforms, including computers, mobile devices, tablets, and gaming consoles.

LET'S START FROM THE BASICS

To utilize Skype, the initial step entails downloading the program onto your device. This can be accomplished by conducting a search for the desired application on the respective **app store** or utilizing a search engine. After completing this step, it will be necessary for you to authenticate your credentials by logging in. In the event that an individual possesses a **Microsoft account**, specifically one with a @outlook.com or similar domain, there is no necessity to undertake the process of creating a new account. Additionally, it is possible to utilize one's personal email address in order to establish the account in a suitable manner. In the event that an account is not already in possession, it is recommended to utilize the **create account tool** in order to establish a new account for personal use.

> *Pro tip*: Remember to check the box that says, *"**Start Skype as soon as the computer logs on**"* to avoid having to enter your password each time you use your device if you want to be connected at all times. Use the remember me option to avoid having to enter your password each time you want to log in, which is another helpful tip.

Checking the Audio and Camera Settings

Make sure the microphone, audio, and video settings are functional before using the program. Since there is a feature to test the audio—microphone and speakers—before you start using, you can do this when you first log in. Do not worry if you skipped this step during setup. Once you are connected, you can continue to do it.

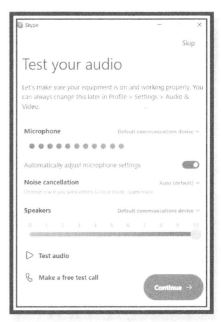

Click on your photo icon above the contacts bar to test and set the settings for your account. There will be a **drop-down menu** where you can select your settings. You can view the necessary information by choosing the **audio and video option** in the settings.

Personalizing the Account

You can further customize your account by adding details like your birthday, the name you want to use, and a picture in the **settings menu.** Access the menu item for "account and profile" to find this information. When you log into the account, you can also choose whether you want to turn off Skype's automatic login feature.

22°C Sunny · Search · W X P A O S T N P · 09:00 AM 01/09/202

Additionally, you can choose your notification preferences, control how the chat menus look, and set your **privacy preferences.**

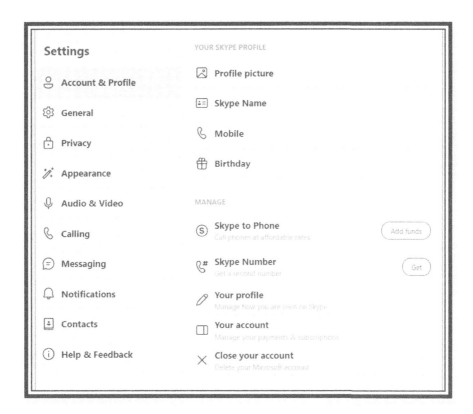

Personalizing Messages

Still in the **settings section**, you can choose a few default actions you want Skype to take when you use it. You might not want the files you receive to be downloaded to your computer automatically for security reasons, for instance. You might also want the chat messages you copy and paste to be marked as quotes. By choosing the appropriate options in the **messaging section** of the application's settings, all of this is possible.

ADDING CONTACTS

You'll need people you can communicate with if you want to install a messaging app on your device. Adding contacts can help with this. It is simple to locate people who have Skype accounts thanks to the software's user-friendly interface. You can use the search feature to look up people you know who might be registered by clicking the search button and entering their name or email address.

When you enter a name, Skype will instantly display a list of the names of those who have accounts in the directory and are the closest to you. The name of the person, the number of connections you share with them, and their location will all be on this list. Since you are just creating an account, it is unlikely that you have had any previous conversations with this person, but you can find all of those conversations under the group chats.

You can invite friends to sign up for a Skype account if you want to talk to them on the service but they don't already have one. The information invite to Skype will appear at the bottom of the results bar if you search for a person's name but are unable to locate them. You enter the person's email address there, and they will get an invitation to sign up for the platform.

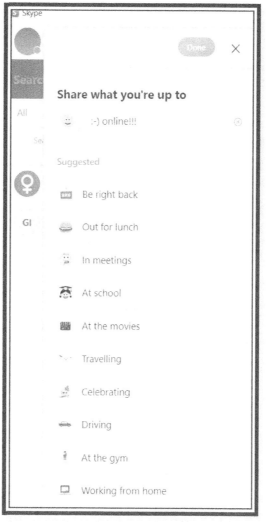

Additionally, you should be aware that Skype will notify you if a user, including yourself, is online or changes their status.

A colored circle will appear next to your icon or the icon of your contact to indicate this.

Click on your image (or the circle with your initials in the top left corner where your name is) to change your active status. Your status is the first choice directly below.

You can choose to be inactive (white), active (green), away (yellow), do not disturb (red), or invisible (grey) when using Skype. Even though you are online when in an invisible status, nobody can contact you unless you first message them.

MESSAGING

When using Skype, you can have one-on-one or group conversations by making video or audio calls and sending messages through chat. It is simple to start a conversation with your pertinent contacts now that you have added them. A new window will open when you click on someone's name in your contacts list to begin a private conversation with them.

You can begin typing your message in the field labeled **"Type a Message"** at the bottom.

In addition, you can start a video message, send an audio message, send a location, schedule a call, create a poll, and send this person a contact that you might have. While speaking with your contact, you'll notice that the window's top has two blue buttons—one with a camera and the other with a **phone receiver**. To switch from messaging to a video or phone call, click on these buttons.

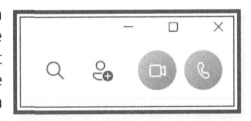

Clicking on the icon next to the contact's name is another way to share this data. You can choose the course of action you want to take in relation to them from a menu that will appear. Additionally, you'll see that a **pencil icon** is present next to their name. By

22°C Sunny   Search   09:00 AM 01/09/202

clicking on it, you can change the contact's name as it appears on your list, add a phone number, take them off, or even block them.

Pro tip: *The only way to unblock someone who has been blocked from your contact list is to access the blocked contacts option under the contacts tab in the settings section of your Skype account. After that, you can speak to them once more after unblocking them.*

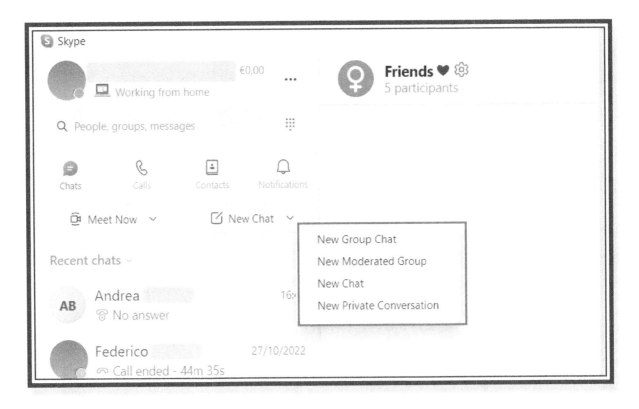

Group Chats

It's possible that you'll want to talk to or message more than one person at once while using Skype, and the program actually makes it very simple to do so. There are primarily two ways to accomplish this. The first involves choosing a contact you want to be a part of the group chat, and then inviting others to join by clicking on the person's icon with a plus sign next to it. This is especially helpful if, for instance, you are talking about a project and would like someone else's opinion or input.

The contacts pane's chats button is where you can also do this. When you do, the options to **meet now or start a new chat will appear.** The type of chat you want to start can be chosen from a drop-down menu that appears when you click the **"new chat" button.** Since this is a group chat, choose this option and include the team members you want to include.

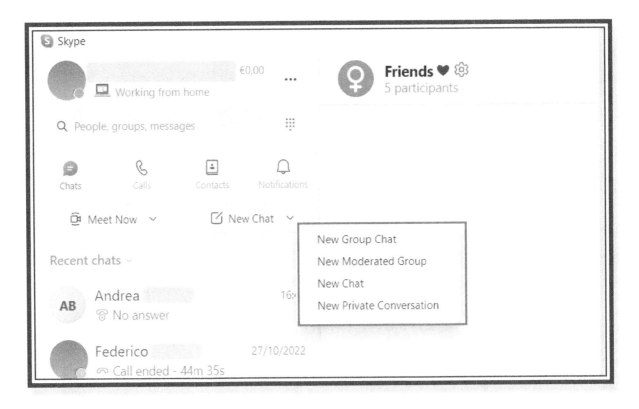

Formatting the Messages

The messaging feature's format and use are the final thing you need to understand. In terms of formatting, Skype does not permit many changes to the text: Use only **bold, italic, or strikethrough to change what you've written.**

Additionally, links may be added (and if you select this option, you may view a preview of the content that will appear in the link). The program will permit you to write code in the message text box if you are a more experienced user. Simply click on the letter **"A "with a pen that is situated to the right of your message box to gain access to these tools.**

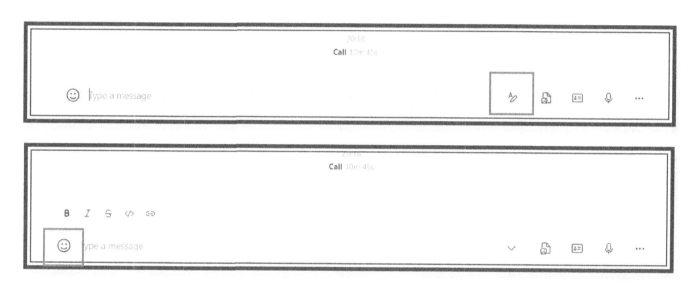

Like many of the contemporary messaging services available today, Skype offers a **selection of emojis** that can be used in various contexts. By **selecting the happy face** to the left of the message box, you can get to them.

When you do, a menu containing a number of available figures will appear, and you can select the one that best suits your needs. If you already know what you want to type, you might also want to use the program's enabled configuration of parenthesis-action-close parenthesis, like (happy), in which case it will automatically figure out what you want to say and return an image.

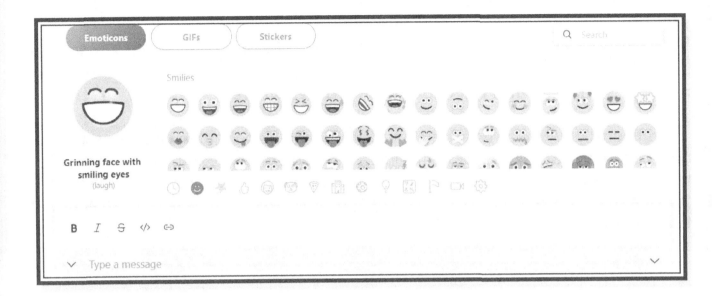

Pro tip: When Skype is installed, the return (Mac) or enter (PC) buttons are usually configured to send a message. If your intention is not to send a message, rather to start a new line of text within the same communication, all you need to do is press the **shift** button and then **enter** or **return,** and you will be directly taken to the next line without needing to start a new message.

KEYBOARD SHORTCUTS

FUNCTION	SHORTCUT ON PC	SHORTCUT ON MAC
View keyboard shortcuts	Ctrl + /	Command + /
Open settings	Ctrl + ,	Command + ,
Open themes	Ctrl + T	Command + T
Open or close dark mode	Ctrl + Shift + T	Command + Shift + T
Search contacts	Ctrl + Shift + S	Command + Shift + S
Next conversation	Ctrl + Tab	Command + Tab
Previous conversation	Ctrl + Shift + Tab	Command + Shift + Tab
Zoom in	Ctrl + Shift + +	Command + Shift + +
Zoom out	Ctrl + -	Command + -
Quit Skype	Ctrl + Q	Command + Q
Start new conversation	Ctrl + N	Command + N
Open contacts	Alt + 2	Not available
Add people to conversation	Ctrl + Shift + A	Command + Shift + A
Send a file	Ctrl + Shift + F	Command + Shift + F
Mark as unread	Ctrl + Shift + U	Command + Shift + U
Search within conversation	Ctrl + F	Command + F
Start video call	Ctrl + Shift + K	Command + Shift + K
Mute or unmute conversation	Ctrl + M	Command + M

Section 7:
Microsoft TEAMS

Microsoft Teams was selected as the optimal option by the corporation to enhance online collaboration and communication among individuals inside organizational settings. While bearing similarities to Skype in terms of functionality, this platform also facilitates online file collaboration, provides the capability to record meetings, and allows for the formation of working teams. Despite the inclusion of the Microsoft Suite in the program, there exists an option to obtain a free download for individuals who choose to acquire it. Microsoft Teams is accessible for utilization on both personal computers and mobile devices.

Upon successfully logging into Microsoft Teams, a chat window will be shown, facilitating communication between the user and other members inside the teams. Adjacent to the window, a set of six buttons can be observed, **including activity, chat, teams, calendar, calls, and files.** The provided buttons facilitate user access to many functions of the program and enable seamless integration with other software applications. In the subsequent chapter, an examination will be conducted on each of these elements and their respective utilization techniques.

22°C
Sunny

Search

09:00 AM
01/09/202

CREATE YOUR FIRST TEAMS

The first thing you need to learn is **how to assemble a team**. This team will consist of individuals who work together on the same project or are on the same team within the organization. Click the team button in the window's left hand panel to start a team. When you've finished, head to the bottom of the window where you'll see a j**oin or create team icon.**

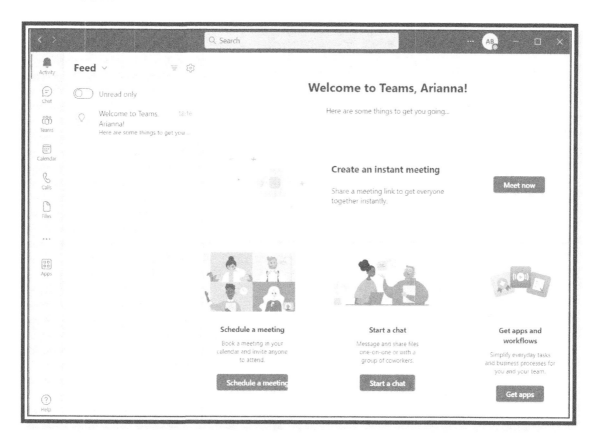

You have the choice to either start a new team or join one once you click on this icon. If you have a code to join a team, you just need to enter it in the window that appears, and **you'll be added to the team right away.** To start a new team, however, you can either do so from scratch or model it after an existing one. Along with these two options, Teams will also give users the option to build a team using a template for **something like project management, employee onboarding, or event management.**

You must first choose whether this team is a **public or private one.** Anyone can join a team that is open to the public, but if the team is private, those who want to join will

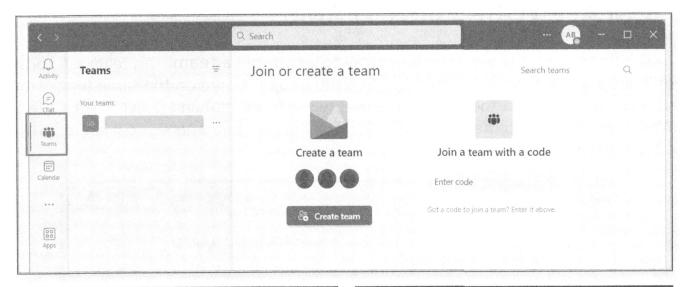

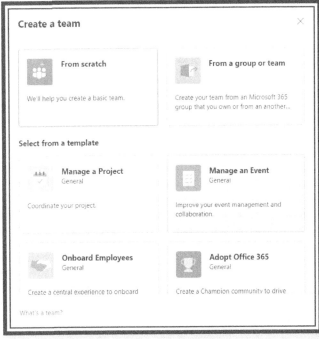

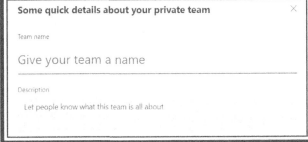

need a code or authorization to enter. You must then choose a name for the team, add a description, and add a data classification after this has been decided.

After everything is finished, you can **begin inviting people** to join the team you created. Click on the ellipsis next to the names of the people you want to add to your team, then select **"Add Member."** If the person you want to invite to a team is not already on your contact list, simply enter their email in the appropriate field, and they

22°C
Sunny

🔍 Search

09:00 AM
01/09/2023

will get an email notifying them of the invitation. **Sending a user the link** to the group that is created after clicking the ellipsis button for the team is another way to invite them to join.

Channels

> ***Pro tip***: *You can identify team owners and their primary authorizations when using Teams. A group may have multiple owners, who may then a**dd or remove members, invite guests, or modify the team's settings.** The group owners will decide on the permissions for the members' and guests' categories of individuals within the group.*

Creating Channels

The team members will be able to communicate about a specific subject through channels. For instance, if you are a teacher, you can set up a channel where your class can discuss homework, another for subject-related questions, and a final one for questions. All members of the groups will have access to these channels, which will enable a better

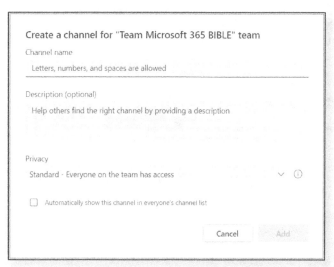

organization of the topics of interest.

Additionally, you will be able to upload files, work together on them, and chat within the channels. Every channel will have a separate chat and file tab, making communication more orderly.

Pro tip: *The activity icon in the left hand panel will turn highlighted whenever there is a **new activity on a channel**. If you click on it, notifications of the groups that have activity or new information will show up. Don't worry if you are unsure of the source of the notification. The details will be highlighted in the window, and you can also see earlier notifications*

Uploading/Attach Documents

Once the channel has been established, you can **upload files** to it so that other users can view them. You can either do this by adding the details to the chat, in which case the document will be uploaded to the **files tab automatically,** or you can go to the files tab and add it directly from there. Along with the option to upload files, this area also gives you the chance to start a **brand-new document** on which users can collaborate.

If the files do not appear automatically, you can click the sync button to ensure that everyone has access to the same data. Finally, users of this channel will have the option to **download the files or create links** to them if they so desire. Users will be able to share or download the document to their devices as a result.

CHATS AND CALLS

Private messaging is also possible, despite the software's primary goal being to foster teammate interaction. Additionally, you can chat with more intimate groups of people. Simply click on the person icon next to them in the chat window's top right corner if you want to add someone else to a conversation you are having with someone in private, for instance.

You can also start a video message **from this screen (camera icon), call the person (telephone icon), or share the screen (icon with the square and the upward-pointing arrow)**.

To avoid switching contacts in the chats while working with multiple windows at once, you can also close a window by selecting the final button on the top bar next to the icon for inviting people.

22°C
Sunny
Search

09:00 AM
01/09/2023
177

Sending Messages and Files in the Chat

If you are familiar with other messaging services, sending messages in the chat is very simple. Teams offers many more options for text formatting than other tools, which is one of its main advantages. The standard bold, italic, and underline features are available when you start typing a message, but you can also change the font's color and style, highlight a particular passage, and even insert numbers and bullet points.

Since they are common across the Microsoft Suite, the majority of the icons are simple to recognize. Using the exclamation point on the tool button to gauge the message's importance is another option. The message box also gives you the option to delete everything at once if you change your mind and decide not to send the message by selecting the trash can icon at the very end of the formatting toolbox.

Message Features

You can mention someone or draw their attention when you message them in Teams by using the '@' symbol. You only need to type "@Anna" in the message field if you want Anna to respond to your message while you are in a channel, for instance. As soon as you click the icon, a list of all the users will appear, and as you start typing their names, the program will filter the contacts until the right person is found. You can click **reply** just below the message to carry on the threaded conversation while keeping the conversation on topic.

You can follow the progression of information because all of the responses to that message will be shown underneath it.

All of the replies to that message will be displayed directly under it, and you will be able to follow the flow of information.

> **Pro tip: Click the "@" button** and type the channel name to message and alert everyone in the channel. The message will be broadcast to all users. Instead of choosing each member individually in your message, you can choose all of them at once.

Sharing files within the message area in Teams is another quick and simple hack. For instance, you must drag and drop the file you wish to share into the message in order to send it in a conversation. All users will be able to see it in the message board, but as an added bonus, it will also be visible in the channel's file section.

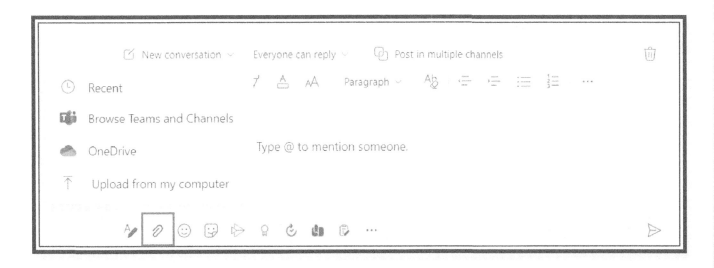

MEETING FEATURES

The **meetings feature** of the Teams software is one of its most comprehensive and intricate components. There are many options available to you when running a meeting through the platform, as you will see in this section. You will discover how to invite attendees, add people, share your screen, change your background, record meetings, and use a variety of other features. Discover what Microsoft Teams can provide for online meetings as you continue reading.

Scheduling and Starting a Meeting

Because Outlook and Teams are a part of the same suite, you can synchronize the data between the two programs to keep your **calendar** up to date with the meetings you'll be attending. In most cases, when you schedule a meeting in Teams, Outlook is automatically updated, making it simpler to manage your agenda. However, since Teams allows you to do it, you are not required to schedule a meeting through the email service.

You only need to access the **calendar icon** on the program's left bar for it to display your availability. To set up a meeting, select the + new meeting button at the top of the window and enter the necessary details. We won't go into great detail because the procedure is very similar to the one you would perform in Outlook. However, you should be aware that you will require a name for the meeting, the attendees, a date and time, and, if applicable, a specific channel. Although it is optional, you can add a personalized text to the invitation.

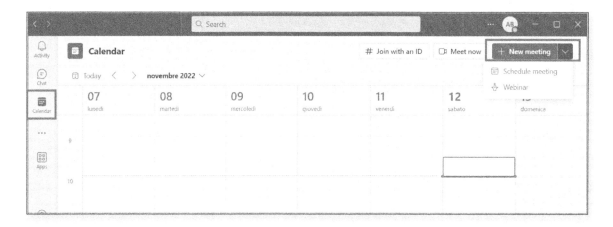

Pro tip: *On the meeting invite's top menu, you can manage the meeting's time zone information and response options. This feature is especially helpful if you are working with people who are located in different regions because it allows you to specify how the invitees can respond and the time for the meeting.*

Once the meeting is near, you will be alerted by the system that it is about to start. If you can, enter the meeting and, if you are the organizer, allow people in the lobby to join the meeting. Once the user clicks on join, they can establish the setting for their video and audio options. They can choose to join without camera and audio. If any of these choices are made, and you want to change it during the meeting, do not worry, You are able to do so once you have entered the room.

If you are in a setting which does not have an adequate background for the meeting, you can also change what the other participants will see. To do this, click on the background filters option at the bottom of the screen where you can see your image.

Once you do, you will be able to choose between blurring the background or choosing some of the standard templates that Teams offers you. Once you have set all this information, it is time to join the meeting by clicking on the join now button on the far right of the screen.

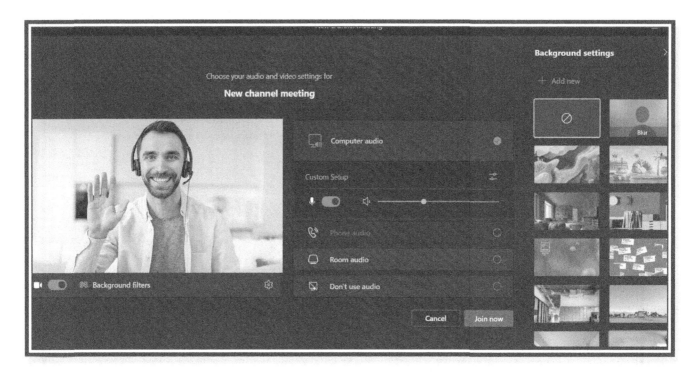

> **Pro tip**: If you use Teams in a professional setting, you can choose to customize your background by adding, for instance, the company logo. To add a new background, select the "add new" option at the top of the background list, then design a unique background using your own template.

You can decide how long the meeting should last and what each participant's role will be while setting it up. You can, for example, allow some users to share their files and screen while preventing others. Manage every option in the calendar's **meeting options** button. It will be easier to establish what each person can do during the presentation, such as removing participants, admitting users in the lobby, and starting or stopping recording, by deciding who will be the **organizer, co-organizer, presenter, and attendee.**

During the Meeting

The participants can use a number of features while the meeting is taking place. Numerous icons that represent various actions can be seen in the window's top bar. The first button will display a list of everyone in the meeting, and the second will show you the chat view.

These tools are crucial because you could find yourself wanting to speak up during a presentation, and you could choose to type it out to ensure that you don't forget. As we saw on the chat, the next button is to raise your hand during a meeting, which is followed by the option to pop open the window.

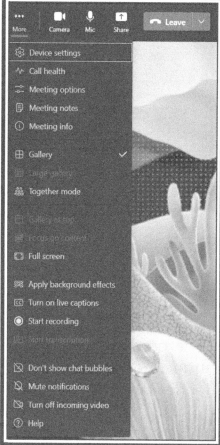

The ellipsis buttons are an essential component of the software, as you may have noticed. If you click on them during a meeting, you will be able to take a number of actions, but only if you are the meeting's organizer.

You have the option of **recording the meeting** as one of these options. When the meeting is over, the information will be accessible in the chat files of the conversation and both the video and the audio can be recorded.

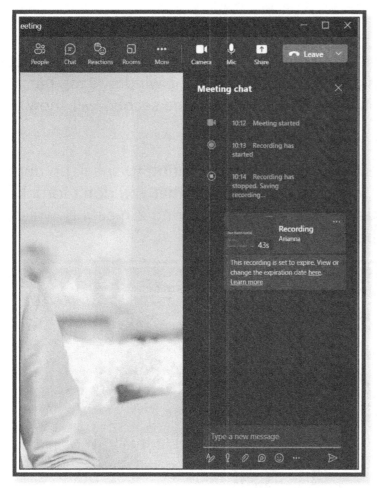

Recording a Meeting

Share content

You can share this externally by downloading the file and uploading it to **OneDrive**, for example, or you can send the link to other Teams users.

The program's accessibility is another nice Team feature. You can use the ellipsis button to enable a **real-time caption** to what is being said because there may be attendees in the meeting who have trouble understanding what is being said.

When you turn on this feature, the program will automatically record what is said and display it for the other users to read. Some languages can also be **translated in real time** in a similar manner, allowing attendees who do not speak the language to participate in the meeting.

It is also possible to change a team member's role in the middle of a meeting. The changes will be made instantly while the meeting is taking place if you simply go to **meeting options.** By selecting the option for meeting notes, you can also **take notes**. You will still have access to these in the chat options after the meeting is over.

The features made possible by the share button are the final ones that need to be covered in a meeting. By selecting it, you can share a window that is currently open on your computer, a PowerPoint presentation, or a **whiteboard** where you can communicate and draw. Users can access all of these features for simpler interaction with the content.

> *Pro tip: Users will be able to view and scroll through a PowerPoint file that you decide to share while you are presenting. The users will only be able to see what you are presenting, however, if you share the file directly from your computer.*

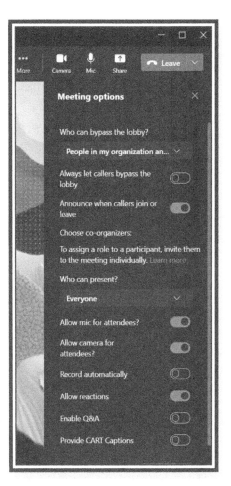

Finishing the Meeting

Teams will give you the option to download a **list of attendees** before you leave the meeting. But before the session is over, this has to be done. There is a distinction between adjourning and adjourning the meeting. **The meeting will come to a close when you adjourn, and the session will be over.** However, the other attendees will be able to carry on without you after you leave the meeting.

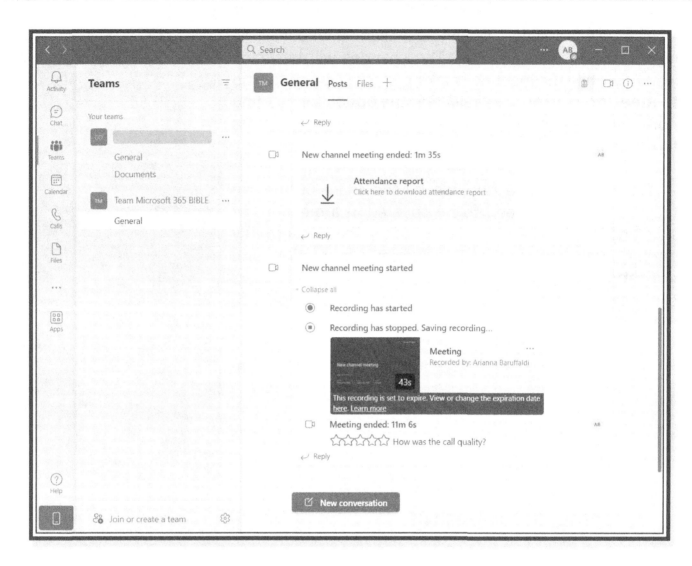

 22°C Sunny  09:00 AM 01/09/2023

Section 8:
Microsoft ONEDRIVE

Microsoft OneDrive serves as the corporate entity's designated platform for cloud-based storage. The cloud storage service facilitates the user in storing various forms of media, such as images, documents, and audio files, thereby enabling seamless accessibility across multiple devices.

Upon obtaining the Microsoft Suite package, users are granted automatic access to OneDrive, a cloud storage service, which initially provides a storage capacity of 1 terabyte (TB). One benefit of the program is that it allows for seamless integration with the user's computer settings, enabling the direct storage of created documents or files in OneDrive without the necessity of saving them locally on the computer.

OneDrive operates in a manner akin to other cloud storage platforms, such as **Google Drive**, while also incorporating certain integrated functionalities specific to Office programs. Continue reading to discover the primary benefits and strategies for leveraging cloud computing to enhance your operations.

LET'S START WITH LOG-IN

To access OneDrive, you can type the program's name in your search engine browser and click on the link once it appears. To login, you will be asked for the email with which you have signed up and the password. This should be the same one you use for all the other Microsoft programs so that it can identify the account and upload the relevant documents.

If you have previously logged in, your password is likely already saved, so you only need to click on continue. You can choose to **enable two-step security** so that each time you log on, a different number will be sent to your phone as an added layer of security. It is not required, but it is advised because you will probably store all of your important files there and may not want others to have access to them.

MANAGING FILES

OneDrive will take you to the **initial screen** when you launch it, where you can see your main folders, files, and other essential data. You can access your files, view recently uploaded or modified items, view photos, open shared documents, and use the recycle bin on the left pane. There is a shortcut to Microsoft's online software for your use on the blue bar directly above it. A task bar that gives the user access to some of the main features of the cloud program can be found directly beneath the blue bar.

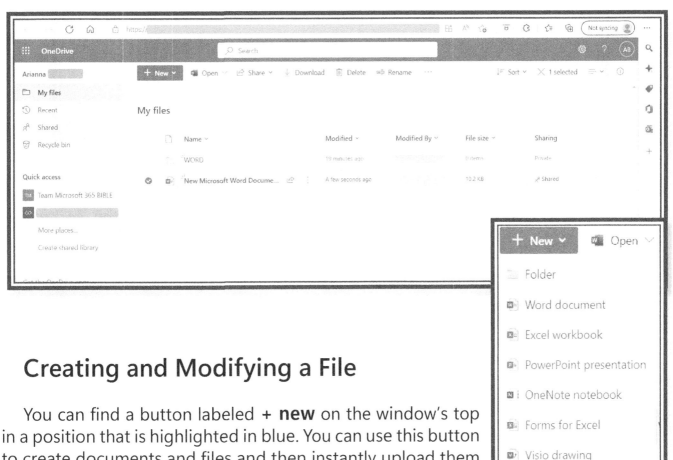

Creating and Modifying a File

You can find a button labeled **+ new** on the window's top in a position that is highlighted in blue. You can use this button to create documents and files and then instantly upload them to the cloud.

OneDrive provides you with the option to organize your files by creating a **Word document, Excel workbook, PowerPoint presentation, OneNote notebook, Forms survey, plain document, or folder.** You can access the online version of the selected software and edit it online by selecting one of these programs. Although there may be some differences between the online version of the software and the version that is actually installed on your computer, the majority of the commands are the same, so you do not need to be concerned. See the illustration below!

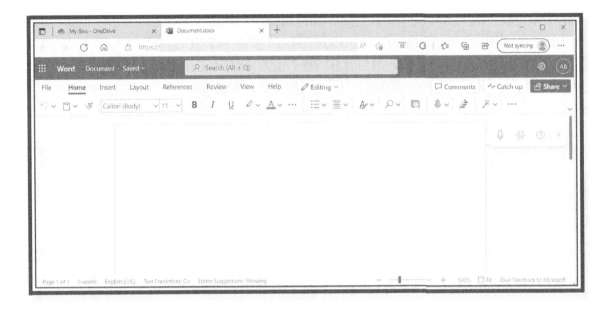

For instance, once the document has been created, it will appear in the workspace's list of my files.

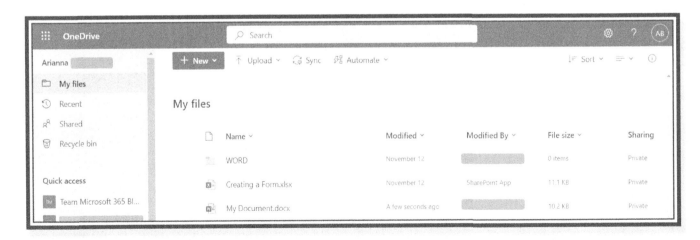

It's crucial to keep in mind that you can create a file in both the workspace and inside of a folder. Click on the file's title (or the hyperlink option) with the right mouse button to bring up a **drop-down menu** with additional options for this file, **including renaming.**

You have the option to preview or open the document here, download or delete it, move, copy, or rename it, as well as view its details and modification history. All of the features in OneDrive allow you to click with the right button, and each file or folder will present you with a variety of options.

> **Pro tip:** *Know the pertinent details concerning your documents and folders. The last time the file was modified, its size, and whether it is a shared or private document are all listed next to the file name.*

Uploading and Downloading Documents

Despite the fact that OneDrive is a program targeted at Microsoft applications, there are no limitations on the types of data you can upload. You can select whether you want to upload a file or a folder to your storage by clicking the button next to the **+ New button on the home page.**

There is a quicker way to do this, though using this feature will let you search your computer for the necessary data before uploading it. You can just **drag and drop** the item into the first page or the appropriate folder if it is already available and ready to upload. You will soon be able to use the archive online as well, and a status bar will show whether it has been uploaded or not.

> ***Pro tip:*** *The drag and drop functionality is accessible across the board in OneDrive. You can use this functionality to rearrange what you have if you want to move files between folders or change the location of something you've stored.*

On the other hand, if you want to **download a document** or do the opposite, you must first select it by clicking the button next to its name. After selecting the document by checking the circle, you'll see that the status bar has been automatically updated with more choices. One of them is the choice to download. When you select it and choose to download it, a dialogue box asking where you want to save the file will appear. According to your needs, choose the appropriate location on your computer.

Other Options

You've probably noticed that the status bar at the top will offer you extra features once you've chosen your desired file. The **share button** is one of them. In the dialogue box that appears when you click it, you can type the email addresses of the people you want to share the file with, add a personalized message, or copy the link to send it through a message. You will notice that the file's **private setting** will change to **shared** after it has been shared, indicating that other people now have access to modify and view it.

You will be responsible for determining the other user's access to the document. It is initially editable when you send the invitation, but it is also editable after the document has been shared. To decide on the fly who will have access to what, click the pen next to the field where you will type the other user's email address and choose between the can edit and can view options.

22°C
Sunny   Search   W X P A O S T N P   09:00 AM
01/09/202

Pro tip: *There is always the option to choose more than one document or folder when choosing. If this is the case, you will observe that the options change once more and that only a limited number of things can be done. When you choose a combination of files and folders, folders and files, or files and files, the status bar will display various action options.*

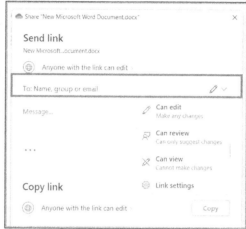

The **</> embed function** is the final choice that you will see in the status bar. You can directly link the data in your OneDrive to any website, personal or professional. The file or folder must be chosen before clicking the embed button. This will bring up a box to the right of your screen where you can add **HTML code to the page.** If you embed a file or folder into a blog post or website, anyone who visits it will be able to view the content without having to sign in. As a result, only publish documents that are secure for you and your company.

SYNCHRONIZATION

As was already mentioned, OneDrive is probably already installed on your computer if you have the Microsoft Suite. When you create a new document, file, or save something on your computer, it will be automatically synchronized with your device if it has been configured with the correct information. Since you can manage these documents online as well, if you choose to do so, you will be able to see the changes when you open the file on your device. With the help of this feature, you can manage your documents remotely and work on them even if your primary device is not with you.

> *Pro tip:* Three blue dashes will appear next to the document's name in the list if there is a new document or a new modification in an existing document in OneDrive.

STORAGE AND BACKUP

The files in OneDrive are already a backup of the data on your device, so you shouldn't need to backup those files. Even if you don't want to regularly have access to air, you can still use it for this. Even if you delete a file from your computer, it will still be accessible in the cloud trash can thanks to this software's intriguing feature.

Let's say you wanted to permanently delete a file from your device, so you chose it and pressed **shift + del.** But when you did that, you accidentally added a file that wasn't meant to be deleted. You won't typically need to worry if the item was stored on your device. Simply visit the OneDrive website and select **the recycle bin** icon on the left. There, you will have access to all the details of deleted files, and by choosing them, you will be able to upload and download them again to your device and the cloud.

Storage

For new users, OneDrive typically offers 1 TB of storage. Check the progress bar at the bottom of the task pane to the left to see how much of this memory you have used. The amount of space you have used relative to the total that is available is shown as a blue line. You will be able to estimate your storage capacity because the information will be both written in words and measurably displayed in the bar.

Pro tip: If you've grown to love OneDrive and would like to purchase more storage for your files, you can do so by going to the options menu and selecting how much extra space you'll require. The recurring payment will be automatically charged each month to the account's linked credit card. Go to the manage and storage icon in the options menu if you'd like more specific information about your storage settings.

ACCOUNT SETTINGS

Your OneDrive account settings are readily available in the program window if you want to view or change them. You can see this view in the top right corner of the window, where your initials are enclosed in a circle. Click this button and choose **"View account"** to access the account information.

You can change your password in this section, check which of your devices have the Microsoft Suite installed, manage your account's privacy settings, including turning on two-step verification, and manage security options.

This section also gives you the option to change or enable different payment methods and view the Microsoft products you have purchased.

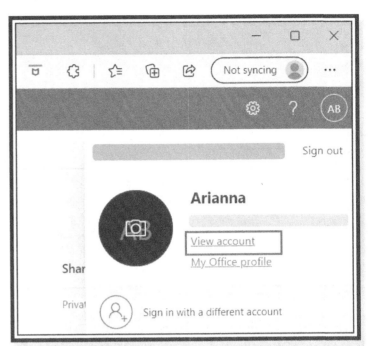

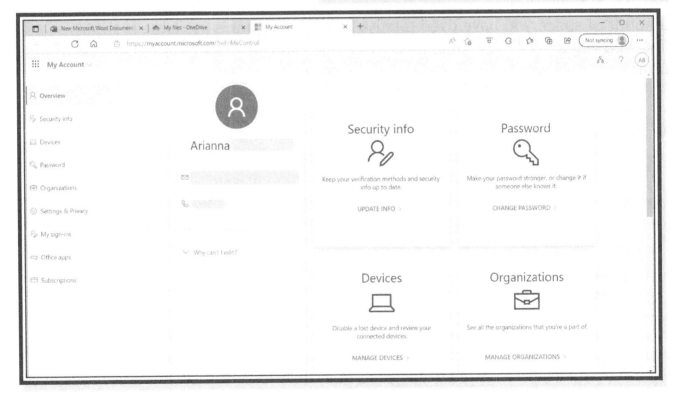

Last but not least, in this part of OneDrive, the user will be able to add family members to their plan, manage Outlook online (without the need to access the original device), and discover other services that are offered by the company.

BONUS SECTION! MICROSOFT FORMS

You've probably noticed that there is one program that we did not mention in the book when you go to OneDrive and are looking to start a new file. **Microsoft Forms** is one such tool. Don't worry if you're wondering what this is. We'll go over this right away in this section.

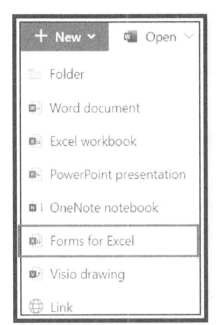

The company's alternative for making online surveys and tests is Microsoft Forms. To conduct a study, for instance, you can personalize your questionnaires here and distribute them to other users. You will always have access to the results because they will be stored in your OneDrive.

Although you can choose a start and end date for the survey or quiz to take place, these will also be updated in real time as the users respond to the questions.

Creating a Form

On OneDrive, **click the + New button** and choose the forms option to begin creating a form. You'll be taken directly to the software's start page in a brand-new window that will open. Despite the fact that using the program is very intuitive, you will learn about some of its key features here so that you can maximize your chances of success.

A new form's first page serves as its blank canvas, where you can enter the form's title and **optional description.** You can explain the purpose of the survey, for instance, to those who will access the form through the description. To edit this data, simply click the Untitled Form name.

CHAPTER 8

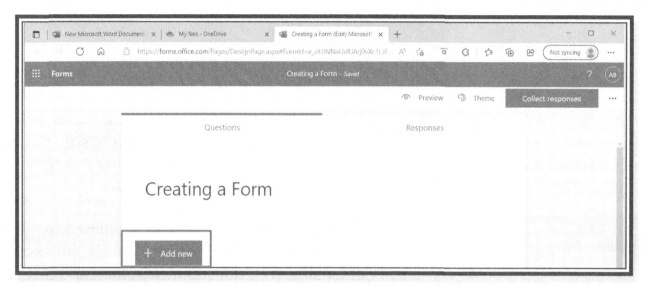

The construction of your form will then begin. You can choose what you want the survey's first field to be by clicking the button labeled **"add new."** Choice, text, rating, and date are all possible variations of this.

Let's assume that you went with choice, the first option. The first **numbered question** on Microsoft forms is generated automatically. What you want to under the options should be added in the question field. After deleting the text, type in the response options you want people to have. If your question has more than two possible answers, click the + Add option button to add more options, or choose this option to add another button.

Regardless of the question, by selecting the appropriate button at the bottom of the box and determining whether this is a mandatory question, you will also be able to determine if the users can select more than one option.

All questions will have access to these choices. If you think the question needs more clarification, for instance, you will also have the option of **adding a subtitle.**

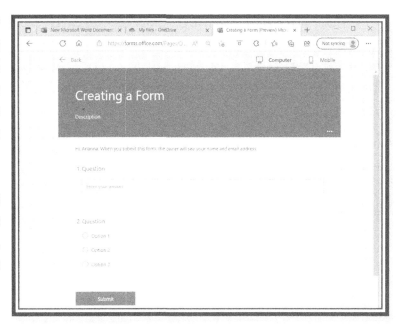

Using the ellipsis button at the bottom, you can reorder the questions as you add new ones to suit your needs. Click the **preview button** at the top of the page to see a preview of your document. By selecting this option, you can also choose a specific **survey theme.**

When you are finished, click the **send button** to retrieve a link that you can send to people you want to participate in the survey. The tab labeled "responses" will be located next to it and contain the results.

> **Pro tip:** *You will be able to download the responses to Excel to further manipulate the data after they appear in graph format..*

22°C
Sunny

🔍 Search

09:00 AM
01/09/202

Section 9:
Microsoft ONENOTE

OneNote is a feature of the Microsoft Suite that lets you keep a notebook and sync your notes with Microsoft Outlook. You can use this software to organize your information in **notebooks, including everything from recipes to work or school-related details.** The program's ability to draw allows you to use your device as a drawing board for any designs you want to create, which is another intriguing feature.

But let's start at the beginning: how to make a notebook and arrange them in the way you like.

CREATING A NOTEBOOK

OneNote will prompt you to choose between opening an existing notebook or starting a new one once it has launched. Let's say we want to start a new one; the first step would be to give it a name. The program will launch to a blank page without the ribbon as soon as the name is decided. The **home tab of the ribbon** should be expanded and pinned to the top of the table by clicking on it.

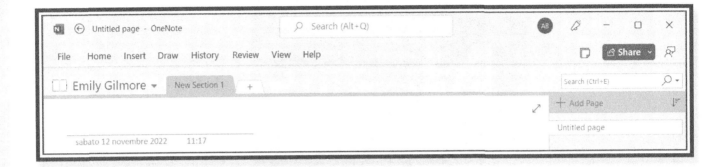

Even though we saw this in the first chapter, let's review: Click on the thumbnail in the task pane's far right corner to pin the ribbon to the window after it has been expanded.

Home Tab

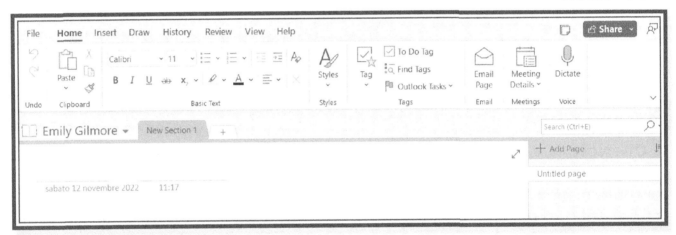

The ribbon is again similar to other programs in the Microsoft Suite, as you will see when you view it for the first time, making it much simpler to navigate. You can paste, cut, and use bullet points or numbered lists in OneNote in addition to the standard font formatting tools. The review pane, which provides the user with translation and spellcheck options, is another feature that is the same.

When you open your first notebook, you will notice that it has a color and a line where you can type the page name. This color tab indicates that this page will be contained within a section. Double-click the section's name and enter the new name in the appropriate field to suit your needs. In this situation, you might want to type in recipes if you are creating a kitchen notebook.

You must type the title of this page on the first line to appear on the page. You can include the name of a dish in the title, to stick with our example. You can add as many pages as you'd like to this section of the notebook by clicking the "add page" button at the top of the pane to the right of your screen. You can add pages to the relevant section by selecting this button.

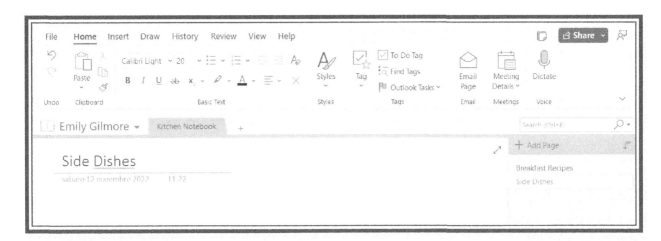

Pro tip: You don't need to worry about renaming the pages because one note will do it for you when you type the page title on the first line that is present.

Creating and Editing Sections and Pages

Let's say you want to add more to this notebook than just recipes, but you don't want the pages mixed together. This can be accomplished by adding a new section. Click the + button next to the first color-coded tab to add a new section. A new section will be created automatically, and the color will be chosen for you. The right button can be used to click on top of the tab and choose the preferred color if you don't think this is the best option or want to change it.

You can also delete the newly created section, export it, or create a new section group by selecting the right button. You can add all of the sections related to a particular area to a new group if you decide to do so. Initially, we were making a notebook for the kitchen, but suppose you want one to keep track of everything about your house.

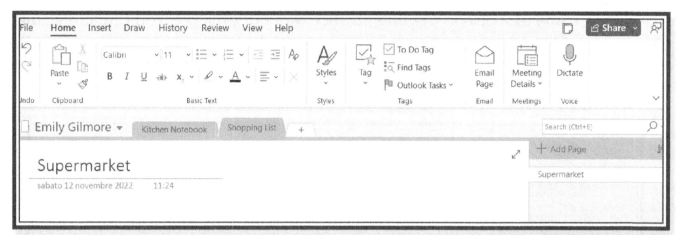

The various areas of the house can be divided into groups, and each group can contain its own specific set of sections. This will show up as a **new section** group on top of the canvas. By selecting the right button, you can rename it as well.

New Section Group

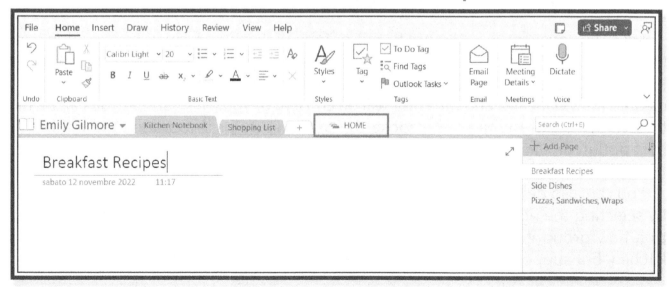

Using Templates and Other Formats

On occasion, you might want to add a particular format to the page you are making. This could be an index card, a to-do list, or perhaps some lecture notes. OneNote has a special feature for this that enables you to use one of the pre-made **templates** to fit your needs. You must navigate to the insert tab on the ribbon and select the page templates button from the pages section in order to access the available templates. The software will let you select from a number of options, and the moment you click your choice, the page will be updated automatically.

Insert Tab

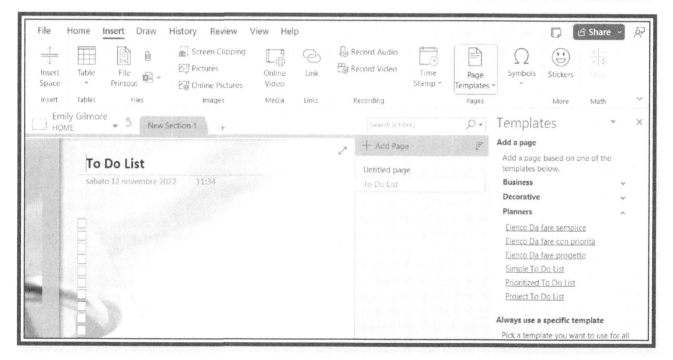

You can add a spreadsheet, a picture, a video, a table, or even equations, symbols, and stickers if you prefer to customize the format on your own. On the insert tab of the ribbon, each of these options can be found in the appropriate section. You can work inside some of these options, including the table and the Excel spreadsheet. Some, like the stickers, are just for show and cannot be modified inside the canvas areas.

Insert Tab

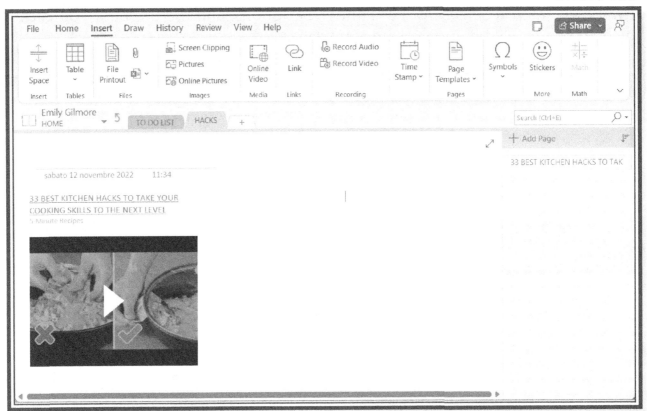

Pro tip: You might not initially be able to edit a picture that you add to the canvas area if it has text on it. OneNote, on the other hand, has a feature that lets you edit and extract data from images. Copy and paste the image into the work area to get started. Once you've done that, use the right mouse button to select the text-copying option by clicking on the image. The extracted text will be moved to another area of the canvas when you click on it, where you can edit it as necessary.

22°C Sunny   🔍 Search   W X P A O S T N P   09:00 AM
01/09/202

Page Settings

Editing your page to remove the title or add lines to the canvas, for example, is not only possible but also has its own section in the ribbon. You can alter the page's color, add rule lines to it (you have a few options to choose from), and even hide the page title under the **view tab of the ribbon's page** setup section. You can **switch the canvas's color to dark mode** using the switch background button, which some users frequently prefer.

View Tab

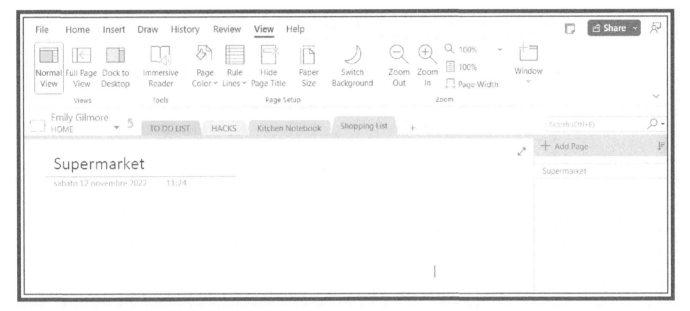

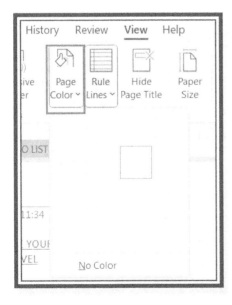

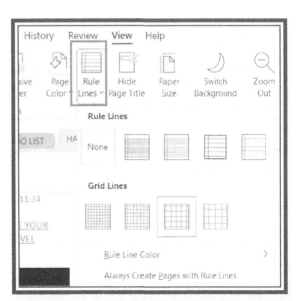

Consider for a moment that you want to print these notes or a portion of the notebook. You can change the **paper's layout** to prevent writing outside the printing area. Go to the paper size button to choose the size of the paper you want to see. A pane will show up to the side of your window once you click on it. It will allow you to select the **paper size**, landscape or portrait orientation, and whether or not margins should be used.

View Tab

You can decide whether or not your choice is intended to be a template by using the checkbox at the bottom of the options. You must choose a name before saving if you want it to be. You can also decide whether this page format should be the norm for all the pages in the section using OneNote.

TAKING AND FORMATTING NOTES

You can begin recording your notes once you've chosen the page's title. While regular text is appropriate for the pages, you might want to use some of the tags to improve the usability of your document. All of the text's quick formats are listed in the **home tab** of the ribbon, along with a **keyboard shortcut** for each one in parenthesis. There are options to highlight your text, write to-do checkboxes, and include icons for passwords, addresses, and phone numbers.

Home Tab

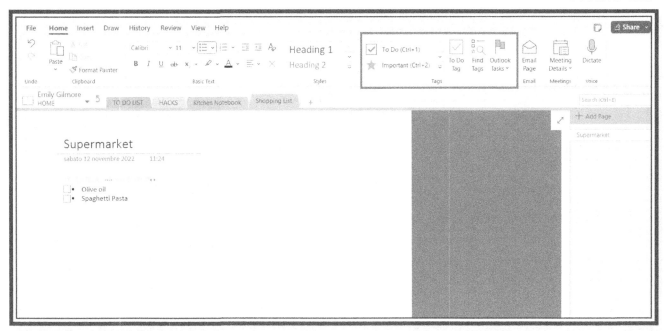

When you choose one of these, it will appear where your cursor was when you last clicked, but you can move it anywhere on the canvas. You can move each option to where you think it is more appropriate by **clicking and dragging it.** Since this is an open area for your creations, you are free to put them wherever you think is most appropriate.

A box will surround the icon after you select it. For more quick formatting and editing options, click on the ellipsis at the top of the text. The dialogue box can be sized to your preference by using the movement arrow. You can either select the quick tag you just made and hit delete, or you can simply click the X button in the **basic text section of the home tab, to remove it.**

Searching for Tags

You can use OneNote to search through your notebooks for any tags you might be looking for. You must access the **find tags button in the tags section of the home tab** in order to do this. You can search for tags by name, section, title, date, or note text in the pane that appears on your screen after you click it. There will be a list of potential tags, and you can select one.

Home Tab

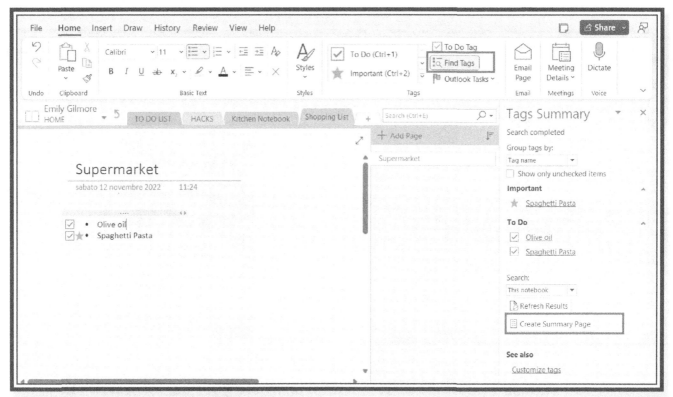

Unless a different option is chosen, the program will automatically look up all of the associated tags in the specified notebook. On the **tags summary** pane's bottom, however, this data can be modified. Here, you can choose to search by time of creation, such as tags created in the last week or yesterday's notes, or by part, such as the notebook, sections, and pages.

Lastly, it is also possible to have an editable list of every tag you have created in one of your notebook pages. You must first decide which page you want to place the list on.

To add a list of all the tags within the selected area to this page, go to the tags summary pane and select the create summary page button. The details of when or where you want the tags to be from must once more be specified.

Customizing Tags

You can **customize** and make your own tags if you believe the ones that are already available are not the best fit for your project. To do this, navigate to and select **the find tags button** from the home pane. The option to customize tags is located at the bottom of the pane. You will see that a **dialogue box** opens when you click the link.

Choose between **adding a new tag or changing an existing one here.** You can click the button if you choose to add a new tag.

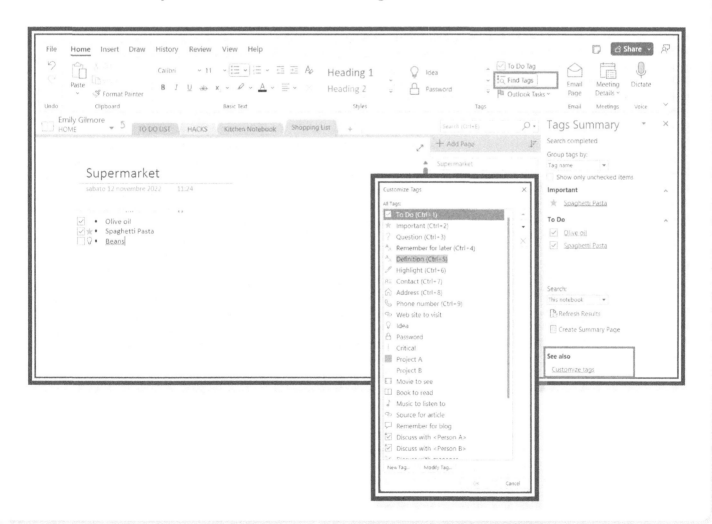

You must choose a name for it, decide if you want to use a particular symbol from the list of options, the font color, and whether or not you want it to be highlighted. You can see a preview of your tag in the window at the bottom of this dialogue box. When you are happy with the outcome, click "ok," and the tag will be generated for you automatically.

Creating Links

The ability to link from one section to another is one of OneNote's best features. The **create links section** that appears when you click the right mouse button makes this possible. The first step is to choose the location on the canvas where you want to put the link. Next, use the mouse to perform a right-click and choose the option link. When you do, a dialogue box displaying every one of your notebooks and sections will appear.

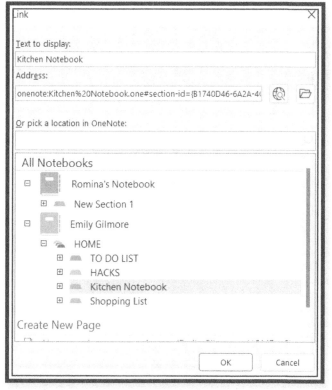

You must type the text that you want to appear in the display. Next, you'll have a choice between two options.

The first step is to select a file or website to link to. This means that you can create links to anything on your device or the internet rather than just adding them to content that was in your notebook. The alternative is to include a link from a different section of an already existing notebook.

To do this, look through the sections until you locate the one you want to use. A page or section from the current notebook or another notebook can be linked here. Only because you will have access to all of your OneNote notebooks in this view is this feature permitted.

Once you've made your choice, click the "OK" button, and the link will be created automatically. Use the **drag and drop functionality** once more to position it where you believe it to be pertinent.

DRAWING AND SKETCHING

When using OneNote on a mobile device, like a tablet, for instance, you'll benefit from the program's **drawing and sketching** features in a number of ways. You can find specific tools to assist you in drawing on the canvas if you click the **draw tab** in the ribbon. It will be especially simple to convert your hand-made designs into something you can register on OneNote when using a pen and your mobile device. *Draw Tab*

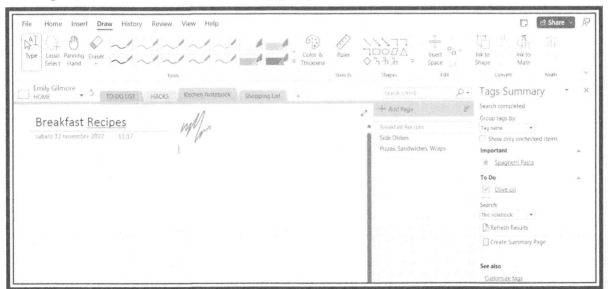

You can manually draw shapes in addition to adding the ones that are already there in the shapes section. You can customize the line's color, thickness, and even whether you want it to be highlighted using the software. Click the **eraser button**, which also gives you the option to select the size you want to use, to remove something you've drawn.

> **Pro tip:** *You can use the* **ink to shape,** *text, or math features to digitalize anything you've manually drawn or written. When you select one of these choices, a new window will open where you can draw the desired shape,* **type the desired text, or write the desired equation.** *The software will then convert it to a digital format.*

RECORDING

The ability to record audio or video using OneNote is one of its additional features. When you do, the notebook will contain these recordings. Go to the insert tab in the ribbon to access this feature. The **recording option** will then appear, allowing you to choose between an audio and a video recording. Consider making an audio recording. In this scenario, the information you want to record will be captured by the device's microphone.

Insert Tab

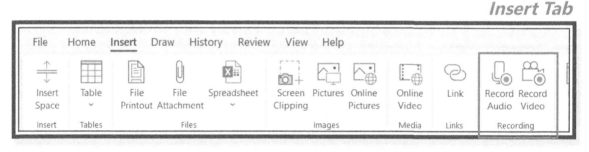

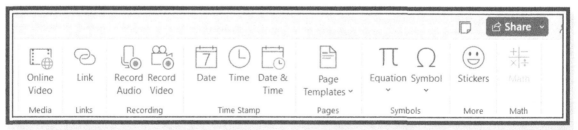

22°C Sunny   Search   W X P A O S T   N P   09:00 A 01/09/202

The moment you click the **record audio button**, an audio recording thumbnail will show up on your canvas. However, there's a catch! This merely indicates that the recording has begun, not that it has ended. As long as you don't press the pause or stop buttons on the ribbon, the device will keep recording. This is important to keep in mind because it is uncommon for the icon to be accessible before the process is complete.

Playback Tab

You may have noticed that a new tab with the label "playback" appeared on top of the status bar in the ribbon when an audio or video file was generated. This taskbar is specifically designed for using OneDrive's audio and video files. You can choose to view or hear the playback, forward the media, and set the settings here. If you clicked on the file tab and scrolled down to the options menu, you would find the same **settings menu** there. The only difference is that you can access the device's audio and video settings directly here. Make sure the camera and microphone are turned on so you can record effectively.

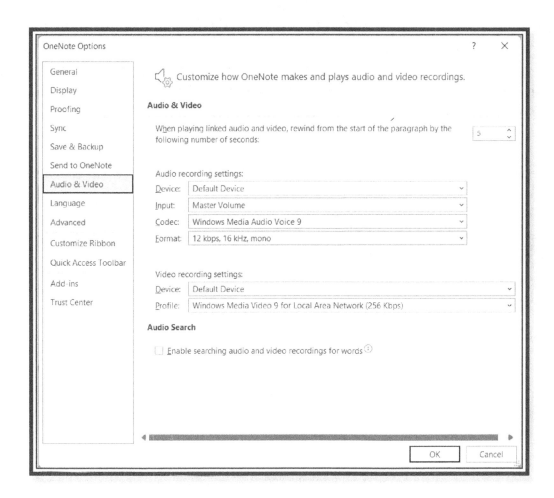

> *Pro tip:* *The page and section pane will be to the right of your canvas when you first launch OneNote. To make it easier for you to work with, you can access the **display option in the OneNote options menu and choose to move the page list to the left.***

SHARING AND SYNCHRONIZING

OneNote can communicate with other programs in the Microsoft Suite, particularly Outlook, which is the last thing you need to know about it. You could, for instance, create a task that syncs with your email software tasks automatically. You must click the **outlook tasks button** in the **tags section** of the ribbon to accomplish this.

22°C
Sunny

🔍 Search

09:00 A
01/09/20

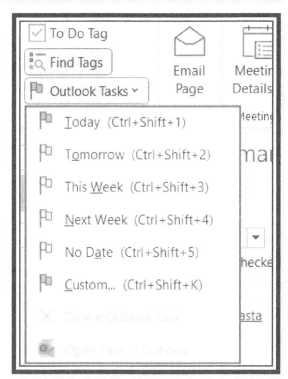

Here, you can choose when the task should be completed (and you can see the keyboard shortcuts for doing so, too).

When you select an option, the canvas will create a flag for the associated tag, where you can enter the task that needs to be followed up on.

After doing this, the same task will be present when you open the Outlook program and select the tasks button. Additionally, a link to the OneNote page where the task was created will be provided.

Pro tip: *You can create a task from* **OneNote to Outlook** *in the same way that you can from Outlook to OneNote. Create one using the OneNote button found in Outlook's ribbon, and the two programs will share the same information.*

You can also email a notebook page to someone else using OneNote. This means that they won't have to read the entire notebook, which might contain sensitive information, in order to see what is written there.

Click the email page button in the ribbon's home tab to email a notebook page. Once you've done that, you'll notice that an email page will open with the page's content in the text body. Use any other Outlook features that you have learned about in Chapter 5 of this book, and type in the names of the recipients.

Send Task on Outlook to One Note

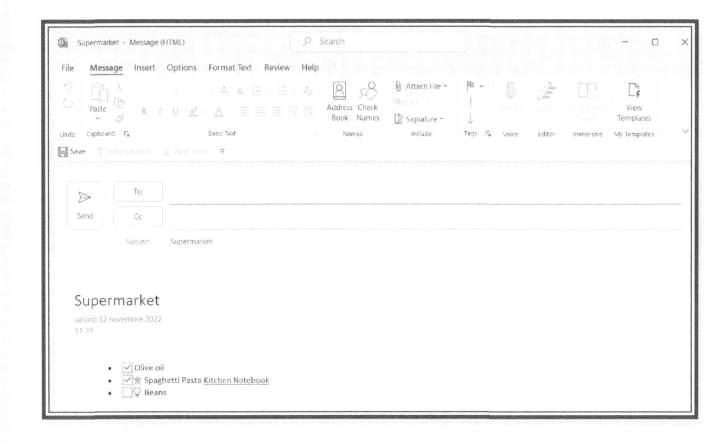

22°C Sunny   🔍 Search   09:00 AM 01/09/202

Pro tip: *Go to the **review tab** of the ribbon to **password-protect your notebook** and stop people from reading private information. There is a yellow padlock with the word password here. To display a password protection pane on your screen, click this button. Click set password to add a password to the page, and it will then be secured. It's crucial to note that if a page or section is protected, you won't be able to search within it until it has been unlocked.*

Review Tab

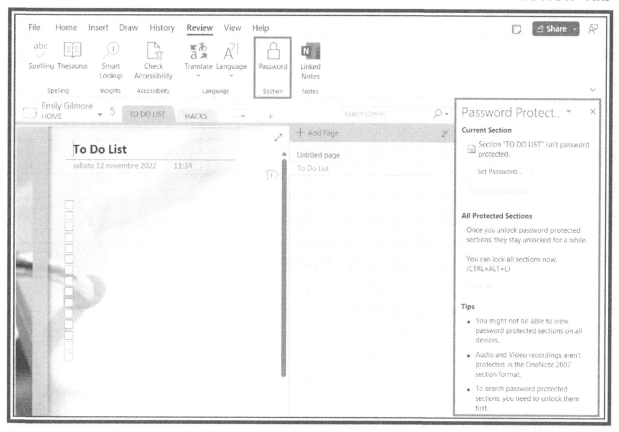

The ability to synchronize your meetings between OneNote and Outlook is the final feature that you might want to be aware of when using these two programs. When OneNote is open, it will instantly update the meetings you have scheduled in Outlook.

The last button in the **meetings section of the home tab, meeting details,** is where you can find these meetings. When you click the button, it will either display the meetings you have scheduled for that day or give you the option to look up other meetings. After choosing the meeting you want to record notes for, click on it to bring up a dialogue box where you can add information. As was already mentioned in this

chapter, you will use the OneNote program here with the added advantage that you can, for instance, take notes and email them to every participant..

KEYBOARD SHORTCUTS

FUNCTION	SHORTCUT ON PC	SHORTCUT ON MAC
Create a link	Ctrl + K	Command + K
Search all notebooks	Ctrl + E	Command + E
Search the current page	Ctrl + F	Command + F
Type a math equation	Alt + +	Not available
Create a new page	Ctrl + N	Command + N
Align paragraph to the left	Ctrl + L	Command + L
Align paragraph to the right	Ctrl + R	Command + R
Show or hide line rules	Ctrl + Shift + R	Command + Shift + R
Insert a line break	Shift + Enter	Option + Return
Start a math equation	Alt + =	Control + =
Close current notebook	Ctrl + Shift + W	Command + Shift + W
Synchronize all notebooks	Ctrl + S	Command + Shift + S
Enter full screen mode	F11	Command + Control + F
Review list of open notebooks	Not available	Control + G
Open other notebooks	Ctrl + O	Command + O
Switch between sections	Ctrl + Tab	Command + Shift + { or }
Insert emoji	Alt + N, S	Command + Control + Space
Insert current date	Alt + Shift + D	Command + D

Section 10:
Microsoft PUBLISHER

As demonstrated in the initial chapter, Microsoft Word has been identified as the optimal software for document creation and text editing. Nevertheless, it is worth noting that Word is deficient in a particular aspect that is effectively addressed by **Microsoft Publisher:** the capability to customize the page layout in accordance with the desired format. The primary purpose of the creation of Publisher is to assist users in configuring invitations, business letters, and cards, as well as facilitating the setup of the page in the appropriate format.

Additionally, it presents itself as a cost-effective alternative to other software solutions with comparable functionality but higher price points. This tool enables users to create magazine layouts and format documents according to their envisioned specifications. Let us examine the methodology by which this task can be accomplished.

SETTING UP THE PAGE

When Publisher is launched and a **new document is opened**, a blank page with blue margins will appear. Your document will use these margins, so anything you want

22°C
Sunny
Search
09:00 AM
01/09/2023
221

to type or paste in needs to fit inside of them. You will find it simpler to decide where to put the **text box** and the images if you use these. In contrast to Word, you must access the margins button on the **page design tab** of the ribbon in order to change the margins of this document. You can also modify the paper size and page orientation in the same section where it is located. Before beginning, configure your page using these buttons.

HomeTab

Page Design Tab

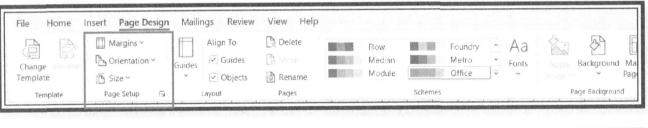

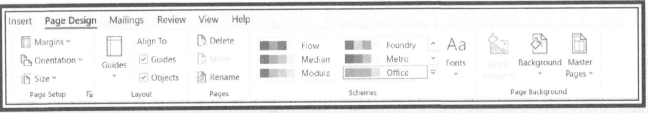

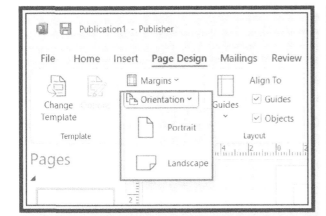

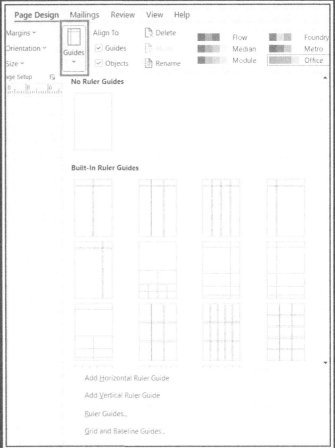

The **grid lines** are another thing you might want to set up before you begin working on the file. In order to put it into practice, imagine that you are making a flyer with information that you want to distribute throughout your neighborhood.

You must set it up so that it looks like a magazine page if you want it to have that format. You can use the **guides button** to properly utilize the layout tools that are offered and avoid having to determine the size of the intervals.

This button will provide you with the appropriate spacing so that you can diagram your page, and it can be found in the layout section of the page design tab. Select the type of guides you want to use in your page by clicking the button. To simplify the design process, Publisher provides a number of options and will let you select one of them.

Here, it's crucial to keep in mind that you shouldn't worry about the margin lines and guidelines printing together because they won't. You should only use this information as a guide.

> **Pro tip:** *Keep in mind that using guides will restrict what you can do inside of them. For instance, text boxes must be contained within them for Publisher to allow you to create one without sending you to the page's edge.*

Although Publisher offers a pre-established format for placing the grid lines, you can also adjust the grid lines to suit your needs. You must click on the ruler at the top or to the left of the page margins to display a grid line. Click with your cursor on the top ruler and drag it down to your page to create **horizontal grid lines**; do the same in the left tab to create **vertical grid lines.**

You will notice that the grid line has been positioned once you have completed this. By clicking on it and dragging and dropping it to the desired location, you can move this line. To better format your document, you can add as many grid lines as you like. If you accidentally added a grid line, you can remove it from the file by clicking on it once more and dragging it out of the page.

Inserting Elements to Your File

The page needs to be set up before you can begin creating. Click on the **draw text box** button located in the home tab of the ribbon to **add text to your document.** After choosing it, you will have the choice of selecting the size that you want for it. To ensure that this box can be properly saved or printed when the time comes, keep in mind that it must be within the grid and margin lines.

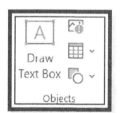

Text Box Tab

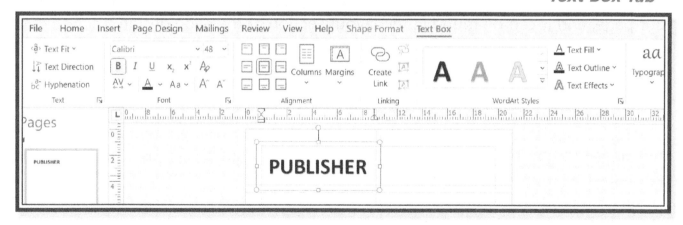

22°C
Sunny

Search

09:00 A
01/09/20

When you release the mouse button after selecting the area where the text should be placed, you will notice that the box has been adjusted to fit the page. Now all you have to do is start typing!

To view the other components that can be added to your publication, go to the insert tab on the ribbon. A calendar, a bookmark to a specific page, a header and footer, specific page borders, and a placeholder for a picture are a few of the standard features that the program offers to the user. Both images from online sources and those on your computer can be added to the document. You can add a placeholder for a picture if you don't yet have the one you want to use.

Insert Tab

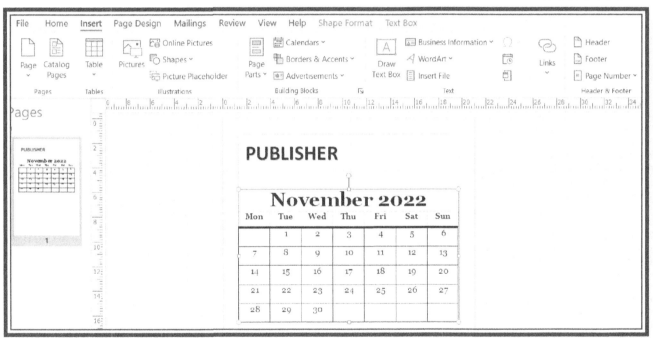

Pro tip: *The majority of the features that Publisher allows you to add are editable. This means that even though it gives you a specific format, you can modify it to suit your preferences and style it with, for instance, the colors of your company or school by clicking the right button on top of these elements.*

You'll see that the **text formatting choices** on the home tab are the same as those found in other programs. You can format the text there to suit your tastes and the way you want to view it. Additionally, you will have a thumbnail view of your pages, just like in PowerPoint.

Home Tab

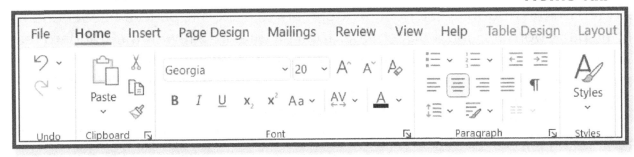

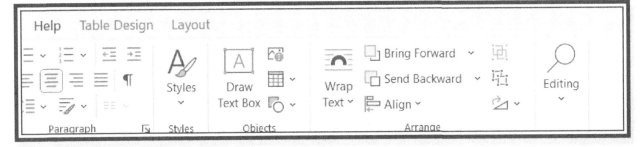

The steps to add a new page are comparable: Select "add page" by clicking with the right mouse button on the thumbnail pane. One of the differences in this situation is that Publisher enables you to view a double page when necessary.

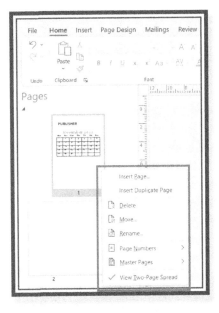

22°C Sunny   Search

09:00 A
01/09/202

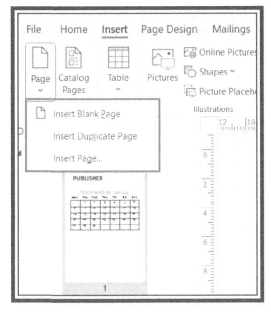

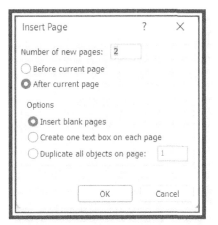

The other method is to navigate to the insert tab in the ribbon, select the page button in the pages section, and then add a single or double page to your document.

Once you click on it, you can decide whether you want a single page or two pages. A dialogue box asking where you want to add this new page will open if you choose the insert page option (the last one). Click "OK" after making your choice. Although the margins will be set as before for these new pages, you must insert the guides.

Pro tip: Go to the view tab on the ribbon and select the single page or two-page spread buttons to see a single page or a double page view.

View Tab

Publisher allows you to enter master pages in accordance with the layout you want for your design, just like PowerPoint does. By selecting the **master pages button** from the page design tab of the ribbon, you can format the default master page, which is **a blank page**, however. Once you've formatted the master pages, every new page you add will adhere to this same standard, giving your document consistency.

You can drag each page in the **thumbnail view,** which is akin to PowerPoint, to change the order of the pages in your document, or you can access the page design tab and click the move button in the pages section. A page may also be deleted or given a new name in this section. When you select one of the choices, a dialogue box asking how you want to rearrange your document will appear. Even if you are unsure, keep in mind that you can change it manually later.

Page Design Tab

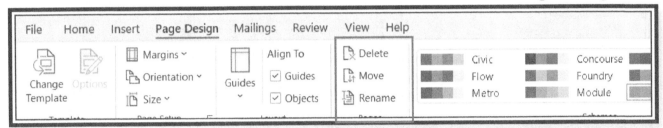

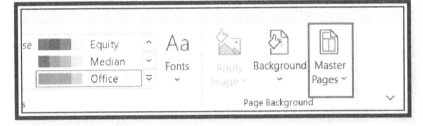

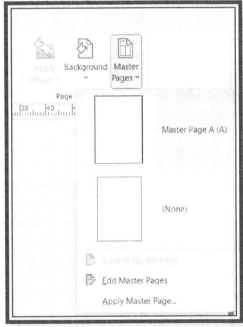

Inserting tables, Word Art, headers and footers, and page numbers are additional similar features that you will notice between Publisher and the other softwares you have already read about. To add images or files to your document, the same steps must be taken. Additionally available in a variety of languages are the spell check and translation features.

Insert Tab

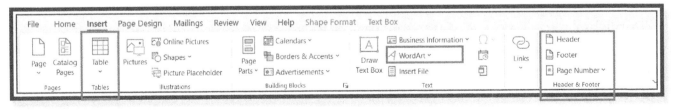

CREATING CATALOGS

A specific tool in Publisher can be used to create a **catalog of the products** you sell if you are a business owner. You should select the **catalog pages** button under the insert tab of the ribbon to begin creating one. A catalog format page will be automatically inserted as a result, and a new tab called **catalog format** will also appear in the ribbon. Create the page you want and add the data you want to your file using this tab.

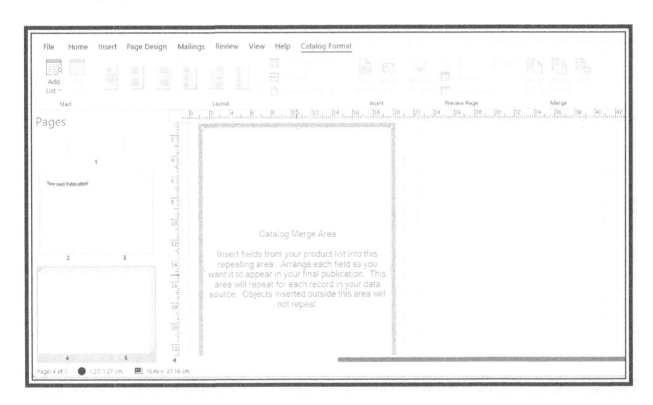

You can place your products in boxes on these pages to better organize the information and present it in a user-friendly way. You can choose the design you want for your file in the **layout area.** Depending on how many products you have, you can choose how many spaces to give each product. You can make a **list of the products** that will be included in these pages so that you can keep track of your information even more easily.

Use the **add list button** on the catalog format tab of the ribbon to create the list. All of the entries for the products you want to place will go here.

You can easily **add, remove, and customize entries** using this tool. You can include the product name, a description, an ID number, a price, and a picture in this list. Publisher will automatically generate a list for you to save and use in your future files once you click the "Save" button.

Pro tip: You will be able to add products to the dialogue boxes you create for the catalog in accordance with the built-in product list once you have done so. The data box containing the pertinent information you want to include will be made up of the list you created. Go to the edit list button on the ribbon to make the necessary adjustments if the list needs to be modified to better suit your file.

If you're making a catalog of items that are on sale, Publisher may be all you need to use to add specific stickers. Look for the advertisements button under the insert tab on the ribbon. When you click on it, a number of sticker options that can be used in your file for sales and other events will appear.

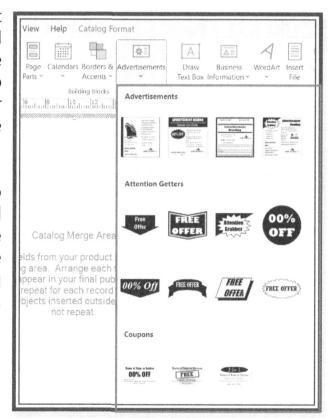

These stickers offer quick access to highlighting a product, though you can still search the internet for other fashionable options. Additionally, by clicking on the image with the right button and customizing it to your liking, you can change its color, font, and style.

22°C Sunny   Search   W X P A O S T N P   09:00 A 01/09/202

CREATING MAILING LISTS

Making an effective mailing system with Publisher is just one of the many advantages of using it for your documents.

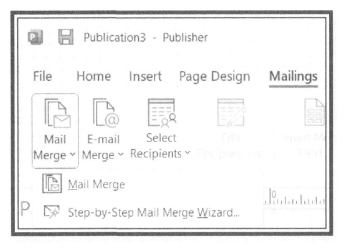

Your publication's information can be personalized or you can **add mailing addresses** using the mail merge tool. You can use the mail merge tool to include both the first and last names of your clients in the document, for instance, if you have a list of their first and last names.

You can either choose to use an existing list from Excel or an Access database, contacts from your Outlook, or you can enter a new list.

Once you've decided on one of these alternatives, all that's left to do is decide where to place the information in your document. You will be given a list that has been personalized so that each of your recipients will receive a message that is specifically tailored to their name. If you have any trouble doing this, you can use the **mail merge wizard**, which will walk you through the process step-by-step.

The creation of an email merge is the alternate choice. While using **the recipient's emails**, the procedure will be similar to creating a mail merge. The same procedure should be followed, and when it's finished, the program will take you directly to Outlook. Additionally, a wizard tool is included with this feature to assist users in managing its use.

Pro tip: *IPublisher will let you type in a list of the message's intended recipients if you don't already have a list of sources you can use.*

*Click the **select recipients button** on the mailings tab and select the type a **new list option** to enter a list by hand. Selecting the edit recipient list button will allow you to make any necessary changes to the list.*

EDITING BUSINESS INFORMATION

In case you need to print the document you are creating for a business, you might want to update the relevant information in the software. Click the file tab on the ribbon to edit your information to make it more accessible.

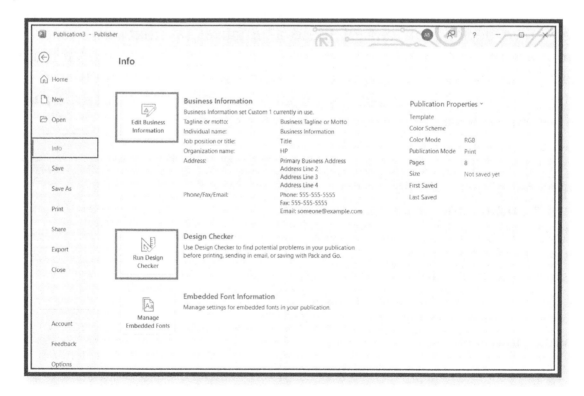

When you finally do, a layout resembling the window that first appears when the software is launched will show up.

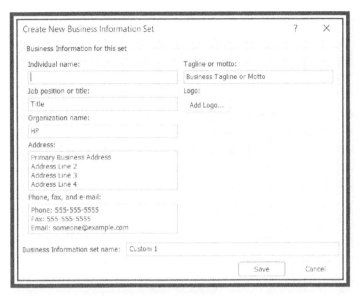

You can edit the business information when you **click the info button.** You can add the pertinent data you want displayed in a dialogue box that will open. A company logo is one of the features that can be included. Once finished, simply click the **save button to finish.**

> ***Pro tip:*** *When you finally do, a layout resembling the window that first appears when the software is launched will show up. You can edit the business information when you click the info button. You can add the pertinent data you want displayed in a dialogue box that will open. A company logo is one of the features that can be included. Once finished, simply click the save button to finish.*

DESIGN CHECKER

The final Publisher feature worth mentioning is one that will enable you to print or save your design without making any mistakes. The **file tab section** of the ribbon's info section has this feature available. Click the design **check button** to verify your design. When you do, a pane to the right of the window will appear and you will be returned to the canvas where you were working. You can run general design checks, publishing checks, website checks, and email checks from this window; the last option is only available for the current page.

> ***Pro tip:*** *The errors will automatically update in the dialogue box as you check each box.*

A dialogue box displaying everything that needs to be fixed in your project will appear below the options from which you can choose the type of check you want to run. Items that are not on the page, for instance, will be highlighted along with the page number where the error is located. White spaces on the page and text that extends beyond the margins are two additional errors that can be highlighted.

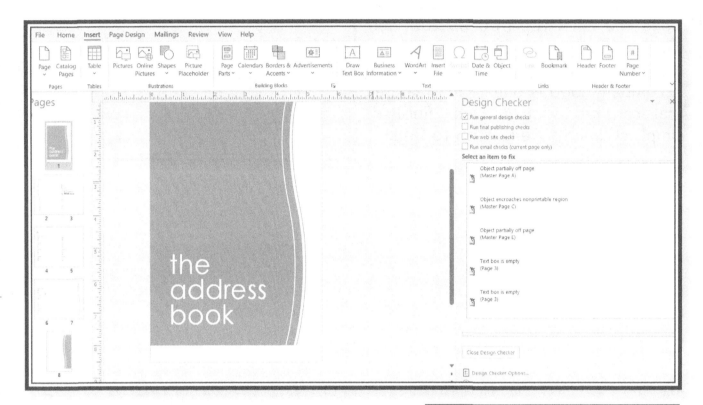

Pro tip: *Go to the dialogue box's bottom and select the design checker options to customize the design check's settings. You can select the page range you want to check, the error type you want to be highlighted, and how the errors are sorted in the dialogue box that will appear. After finishing, you can run the design checker once more.*

Conclusion

The completion of this tutorial signifies the acquisition of comprehensive knowledge required for proficient utilization of the Microsoft Office suite. Throughout the course of this literary work, readers have been exposed to the techniques and procedures involved in generating and structuring textual content using the Microsoft Word application, as well as the principles and strategies for effectively handling data within the Microsoft Excel software. The acquisition of skills in designing impactful presentations using PowerPoint and effectively managing email correspondence through Outlook has been achieved. The utilization of these four fundamental tools is imperative for individuals seeking to advance their proficiency with the software, particularly within a corporate setting.

However, that was not the extent of the matter. The user has demonstrated proficiency in database creation using Microsoft Access, as well as communication skills through chat and call functionalities in Skype and Teams. Furthermore, the user has exhibited knowledge in utilizing secure storage solutions such as OneDrive for document management. In addition, the user has gained insight into the fundamental aspects of constructing forms within Microsoft Forms and the potential benefits they offer for conducting polls and surveys.

In conclusion, the aforementioned discussion has elucidated the process of managing notes in OneNote and constructing proficient layouts in Publisher.

Congratulations on your achievement! Your understanding of the functionality of these tools appears to be commendable. It is important to note that when using various software applications, many of them exhibit similar organizational structures and utilize identical icons for their respective tools. This commonality facilitates ease of navigation across different software platforms. The ribbon interface is a ubiquitous feature found in nearly all software applications, and acquiring proficiency in its usage can greatly enhance one's productivity and effectiveness in accomplishing various tasks.

I trust that this book has proven to be beneficial in resolving any uncertainties you may have had concerning these programs. Furthermore, as an additional advantage, the keyboard shortcuts associated with each program are presented at the conclusion of each section. Nevertheless, similar to numerous other functionalities found in these software applications, the majority of them will exhibit a commonality, including the widely recognized copy and paste feature (Ctrl + C and Ctrl + V). Utilize these tools to optimize your user experience and streamline the file creation process, thereby saving valuable time.

Ultimately, it is my desire that you retain this book as a valuable reference guide, readily accessible for consultation as the need arises. The primary objective of this book was to serve as a comprehensive resource for learning and reference purposes, particularly to address uncertainties or lapses in memory. In the event that one finds it necessary to revisit a particular section of text for the purpose of comprehension or clarification, it is advisable to consult the corresponding chapter and engage in a rereading exercise without hesitation. The majority of the information is expected to remain unaltered despite potential software updates. It is expected that users will experience a sense of security when utilizing this software, and the knowledge acquired through its usage is anticipated to be beneficial for their future pursuits, whether in personal or professional domains.

If readers have found this book to be enjoyable and believe that its content has enhanced their comprehension of program management in their everyday lives, we kindly request that they share their thoughts and feedback by leaving a review and comment. These contributions will be highly valued and will contribute to the enhancement of forthcoming content. **Wishing you the best of luck!**

Index

22°C Sunny

Search

09:00 A
01/09/202

22°C
Sunny

🔍 Search

09:00 AM
01/09/2023

239

22°C Sunny   Search   09:00 A 01/09/20

Shortcut Features 13

22°C
Sunny
Search
09:00 AM
01/09/2023
241

References

Academy Pop. (2019a, November 9). *PowerPoint de office 365 - Curso desde 2019.* Www.youtube.com. https://www.youtube.com/watch?v=mqB3cIPlniU

Academy Pop. (2019b, November 9). *PowerPoint de office 365 - Curso desde cero.* Www.youtube.com. https://www.youtube.com/watch?v=8Af21eIrhvl

Albinagorta, C. (2020, January 16). *PowerPoint 101: The ultimate tutorial for beginners.* 24slides.com. https://24slides.com/presentbetter/powerpoint-101-the-ultimate-tutorial-for-beginners

Basu, S. (2019, May 21). *10 hidden features of Microsoft Word that'll make your life easier.* MakeUseOf. https://www.makeuseof.com/tag/10-hidden-microsoft-word-features-will-make-life-easier/

Blaga, M. M. (2016, September 30). *5 Things you can do with the OneDrive app from the Windows Store.* Digital Citizen. https://www.digitalcitizen.life/5-things-you-can-do-onedrive-app-windows-store/

Boudrie, S. (2016). Office 365 OneDrive Tutorial. In *You Tube*. https://www.youtube.com/watch?v=jzo4Pjt7g18

CFI Team. (2022a, June 7). *Rate function*. Corporate Finance Institute. https://corporatefinanceinstitute.com/resources/excel/functions/rate-function/

CFI Team. (2022b, June 12). *Yield function*. Corporate Finance Institute. https://corporatefinanceinstitute.com/resources/excel/functions/yield-function/

Childress, A. (2019, January 18). *How to learn PowerPoint quickly (complete beginner's guide)*. Business Envato Tuts+. https://business.tutsplus.com/tutorials/how-to-learn-powerpoint--cms-29884

CMIT Solutions. (2018, January 30). *Top 10 Microsoft Outlook tips to maximize efficiency*. CMIT Solutions. https://cmitsolutions.com/blog/top-10-microsoft-outlook-tips/

Collaboration Coach. (2020, January 14). *A beginners guide to Microsoft OneNote*. www.youtube.com. https://www.youtube.com/watch?v=JEJZbjcMkeU

Competitive Computer Consultants Inc. (2020). Learn OneDrive in 12 Minutes. In *You Tube*. https://www.youtube.com/watch?v=b2bqPtX3tfc

Escuela Directa. (2021, October 4). *Tutorial de Microsoft Access desde Cero en 2 Horas*. You Tube. https://www.youtube.com/watch?v=b-j7K9YPQil

Find Easy Solution. (2020). How to create a presentation in PowerPoint - Office 365. In *YouTube*. https://www.youtube.com/watch?v=abm6GxlbRgE

Fisher, T. (2022, July 11). *Microsoft Publisher tutorial for beginners*. Lifewire. https://www.lifewire.com/microsoft-publisher-basics-4138207

FreecodeCamp.org. (2020, October 28). *Microsoft Excel tutorial for beginners - full course*. YouTube. https://www.youtube.com/watch?v=Vl0H-qTclOg

GCF Learn Free. (2019, June 21). *Microsoft Access*. You Tube. https://www.youtube.com/playlist?list=PLpQQipWcxwt-EHfE5zXtUrLtFYnOPBRE_

Gharani, L. (2021a). How to use Microsoft Teams effectively | Your complete guide. In *YouTube*. https://www.youtube.com/watch?v=z6IUiamE3-U

Gharani, L. (2021b). Excel Tutorial for beginners | Excel made easy. In *YouTube*. https://www.youtube.com/watch?v=0tdlR1rBwkM

Gralla, P. (2021, February 10). *PowerPoint for Microsoft 365 cheat sheet*. Computerworld. https://www.computerworld.com/article/3606749/powerpoint-for-microsoft-365-cheat-sheet.html

Guru99. (2020, March 25). *MS Access tutorial: Learn with example*. Guru99. https://www.guru99.com/ms-access-tutorial.html

Indeed Editorial Team. (2022, May 31). *5 basic Excel skills and how to include them in your resume*. Indeed Career Guide. https://ca.indeed.com/career-advice/resumes-cover-letters/basic-excel-skills

Indigorafa. Indigo Tutoriales. (2011). Tutorial Excel (Cap. 1) Conocimientos basicos. In *YouTube*. https://www.youtube.com/watch?v=hrCOOF_z6mc

InvestInTech. (2019, August 7). *A quick beginner's guide to Microsoft Publisher*. PDF Blog | Investintech PDF Solutions. https://www.investintech.com/resources/blog/archives/9269-microsoft-publisher-beginners-guide.html

Kaceli TechTraining. (n.d.). *Access 2019 full tutorial: Microsoft Access made easy*. You Tube. Retrieved October 16, 2022, from https://www.youtube.com/watch?v=C7oCwdm_wXg

Kover. (2018). Skype Video Call Tutorial. In *YouTube*. https://www.youtube.com/watch?v=TgcEfK6wCTo

Kumar, A. (2019, January 26). *History & evolution of Microsoft Office software*. The Windows Club. https://www.thewindowsclub.com/history-evolution-microsoft-office-software

Learnit Training. (2020). Word beginner tutorial. In *YouTube*. https://www.youtube.com/watch?v=yV4i29Xo0iM

Learnit Traning. (n.d.). OneDrive for business tutorial. In *You Tube*. Retrieved July 23, 2021, from https://www.youtube.com/watch?v=vMFYFz-emlw

M, S. (2020, September 8). *50 best keyboard shortcuts in Excel you should know in 2022-23*. Simplilearn. https://www.simplilearn.com/tutorials/excel-tutorial/excel-shortcuts

Majors, H. (2022). Use OneNote effectively and stay organized. In *You Tube*. https://www.youtube.com/watch?v=ZridMFj3Rzc

Michaloudis, J. (2022, March 26). *Introduction to Microsoft Word 365 tutorial*. My Excel Online. https://www.myexcelonline.com/blog/introduction-to-microsoft-word-365/

Microsoft Support. (n.d.-a). *Basic tasks in Excel*. Microsoft. Retrieved October 6, 2022, from https://support.microsoft.com/en-us/office/basic-tasks-in-excel-dc775dd1-fa52-430f-9c3c-d998d1735fca

Microsoft Support. (n.d.-b). *Basic tasks in Publisher*. Microsoft Support. Retrieved October 17, 2022, from https://support.microsoft.com/en-us/office/basic-tasks-in-publisher-0e5ed249-1927-433f-a35c-63beb8216fcf

Microsoft Support. (n.d.-c). *Keyboard shortcuts for Access*. Support.microsoft.com. https://support.microsoft.com/en-us/office/keyboard-shortcuts-for-access-70a673e4-4f7b-4300-b8e5-3320fa6606e2

Microsoft Support. (n.d.-d). *Keyboard shortcuts for Outlook*. Support.microsoft.com. https://support.microsoft.com/en-us/office/keyboard-shortcuts-for-outlook-3cdeb221-7ae5-4c1d-8c1d-9e63216c1efd

Microsoft Support. (n.d.-e). *Keyboard shortcuts in OneNote*. Support.microsoft.com. Retrieved October 17, 2022, from https://support.microsoft.com/en-us/office/keyboard-shortcuts-in-onenote-44b8b3f4-c274-4bcc-a089-e80fdcc87950

Microsoft Support. (n.d.-f). *Keyboard shortcuts in Publisher*. Microsoft Support. Retrieved October 17, 2022, from https://support.microsoft.com/en-us/office/keyboard-shortcuts-in-publisher-289f9c39-5584-49f0-b9a9-081e646152ea

Microsoft Support. (n.d.-g). *Keyboard shortcuts in Word*. Support.microsoft.com.

https://support.microsoft.com/en-us/office/keyboard-shortcuts-in-word-95ef89dd-7142-4b50-afb2-f762f663ceb2#PickTab=macOS

Microsoft Support. (n.d.-h). *Microsoft Teams video training*. Microsoft Support. https://support.microsoft.com/en-us/office/microsoft-teams-video-training-4f108e54-240b-4351-8084-b1089f0d21d7

Microsoft Support. (n.d.-i). *OneDrive video training*. Microsoft Support. https://support.microsoft.com/en-us/office/onedrive-video-training-1f608184-b7e6-43ca-8753-2ff679203132

Microsoft Support. (n.d.-j). *Use keyboard shortcuts to deliver PowerPoint presentations*. Support.microsoft.com. https://support.microsoft.com/en-us/office/use-keyboard-shortcuts-to-deliver-powerpoint-presentations-1524ffce-bd2a-45f4-9a7f-f18b992b93a0

My e-lessons. (2014, July 14). *10 most used formulas MS Excel*. YouTube. https://www.youtube.com/watch?v=KyMj8HEBNAk

MyExcelOnline.com. (2022, March 8). *Microsoft Outlook tutorial for beginners in 2022*. Www.youtube.com. https://www.youtube.com/watch?v=pWGtXWumb4A

Online Training for Everyone. (n.d.). Microsoft Word advanced tutorial. In *YouTube*. Retrieved September 25, 2022, from https://www.youtube.com/watch?v=9AFusrHbK6A

Plain Concepts. (2022, June 20). *Tutorial Microsoft Teams*. Plain Concepts. https://www.plainconcepts.com/tutorial-microsoft-teams/

Sartain, J. (2019, December 29). *Your Excel formulas cheat sheet: 22 tips for calculations and common tasks*. PCWorld. https://www.pcworld.com/article/431558/excel-formulas-cheat-sheet-15-essential-tips-for-calculations-and-common-tasks.html

Simon Sez IT. (n.d.). *Microsoft PowerPoint for beginners: 4-hour training course in PowerPoint 2021/365*. Www.youtube.com. Retrieved October 14, 2022, from https://www.youtube.com/watch?v=LEe8OKhfJWw

Simon Sez IT. (2021a). OneNote tutorial: Getting started with Microsoft OneNote. In *You Tube*. https://www.youtube.com/watch?v=k9eIwXXJyss

22°C
Sunny
Search
09:00 A
01/09/202

Simon Sez IT. (2021b). Microsoft Word advanced tutorial - Microsoft Word tips and tricks. In *YouTube*. https://www.youtube.com/watch?v=xT3gMWjQzdE

Skills Factory. (n.d.). Microsoft Word - Tutorial for beginners in 13 minutes. In *YouTube*. Retrieved September 25, 2022, from https://www.youtube.com/watch?v=GBHUBEOTdcA

Stratvert, K. (2021, February 25). *How to use Microsoft Access - beginner tutorial*. You Tube. https://www.youtube.com/watch?v=ubmwp8kbfPc

Sung, D. (2021, March 30). *How to use Skype: A beginner's guide for complete Skype novices*. Pocket Lint. https://www.pocket-lint.com/apps/news/skype/113286-how-to-use-skype

Teacher's Tech. (2021a). How to use Microsoft Outlook - Tutorial for beginners. In *YouTube*. https://www.youtube.com/watch?v=UcikK-9oP00

Teacher's Tech. (2021b, November 28). *Microsoft Access tutorial - beginners level 1 (quick start)*. YouTube. https://www.youtube.com/watch?v=Sxp8YjKu_Tc

Techboomers. (2017). How to Use Skype. In *YouTube*. https://www.youtube.com/watch?v=S38e-t6rhKA

Technology for Teachers and Students. (2018). The Beginner's Guide to Microsoft Publisher. In *YouTube*. https://www.youtube.com/watch?v=Cqo0PVhBFYI

Technology for Teachers and Students. (2019a). Beginner's guide to Microsoft Outlook - 2019 Tutorial. In *YouTube*. https://www.youtube.com/watch?v=WfSCfBntqPU

Technology for Teachers and Students. (2019b). Beginner's guide to OneDrive for Windows - Updated tutorial. In *YouTube*. https://www.youtube.com/watch?v=hkf1p1Y6rFQ

Tholfsen, M. (2021, January 26). Top 20 Microsoft Outlook tips and tricks [2021] all the Outlook features you didn't know about! Www.youtube.com. https://www.youtube.com/watch?v=RyPPL6gGvj4

Wikipedia Contributors. (2019, April 20). *Skype*. Wikipedia; Wikimedia Foundation. https://en.wikipedia.org/wiki/Skype

Made in the USA
Las Vegas, NV
24 October 2023

79610091R10136